The Original 1939
Notebook of a Return to the Native Land

publication of this book is funded by the
Beatrice Fox Auerbach Foundation Fund
at the Hartford Foundation for Public Giving

AIMÉ CÉSAIRE

THE ORIGINAL 1939
NOTEBOOK OF A RETURN
TO THE NATIVE LAND

BILINGUAL EDITION

TRANSLATED AND EDITED BY

A. JAMES ARNOLD AND
CLAYTON ESHLEMAN

WESLEYAN UNIVERSITY PRESS
MIDDLETOWN, CONNECTICUT

Wesleyan University Press
Middletown CT 06459
www.wesleyan.edu/wespress
© 2013 by A. James Arnold and Clayton Eshleman
French text © 1939 The Estate of Aimé Césaire
All rights reserved
First paperback edition 2023
ISBN for the paperback edition 978-0-8195-0066-3
Manufactured in the United States of America
Original art by Wifredo Lam, used by permission of Eskil Lam

Publication of this book is funded by the
Beatrice Fox Auerbach Foundation Fund
at the Hartford Foundation for Public Giving

The Library of Congress cataloged the hardcover edition as:
Césaire, Aimé.
The original 1939 notebook of A return to the native land :
bilingual edition / Aimé Césaire ; translated and edited
by A. James Arnold and Clayton Eshleman.
pages cm. — (Wesleyan poetry series)
In English and French.
Original French text published under title:
Cahier d'un retour au pays natal.
Includes bibliographical references.
ISBN 978-0-8195-7370-4 (cloth : alk. paper)
ISBN 978-0-8195-7371-1 (ebook)
I. Arnold, A. James (Albert James), 1939- translator editor.
II. Eshleman, Clayton, translator editor. III. Césaire, Aimé.
Poems. Selections. IV. Césaire, Aimé. Poems. Selections.
English. V. Title.
PQ3949.C44C3413   2013
841'.914—dc23
2013002821

5 4 3 2 1

à Wifredo Lam
en témoignage d'amitié
et d'admiration

a poème de nos révoltes,
de nos espoirs,
de notre ferveur.

Fort-de-France
mai 1941.

A. Césaire

CE TEXTE A ÉTÉ PUBLIÉ
POUR LA PREMIÈRE FOIS
PAR VOLONTÉS
REVUE MENSUELLE
8bis, BD DE COURCELLES
PARIS 17ᵉ

TIRAGE A PART
LIMITÉ A 50 EXEMPLAIRES.

Césaire dedication of offprint to Wifredo Lam

à Wifredo Lam	to Wifredo Lam
en témoignage d'amitié	in token of friendship
et d'admiration	and admiration
ce poème de nos révoltes,	this poem of our revolts,
de nos espoirs,	our hopes,
de notre ferveur.	our fervor.
Fort-de-France	Fort-de-France
mai 1941	May 1941
———————	———————
A. Césaire	A. Césaire

Contents

whose purpose has been reoriented by later modifications. A remarkable characteristic of the text is Césaire's use of the French alexandrine line of verse. French prosody is arithmetically, rather than metrically, conventional. It does not rely on classical meter derived from Greek or Latin. The alexandrine is so culturally ingrained that the French ear picks it up unselfconsciously.[1] In the 1939 text the interjection of an isolated alexandrine line of verse signals an important shift in focus through rhythmic modulation. Alexandrines can be found at strophes 37, 53, and 63 (twice in the second sequence and at the beginning of the third). We have attempted to approximate this effect by using a greater solemnity, more formal lexical choices, or unusual syntax in translating those same lines. There is no conventional meter we can use to achieve the identical effect.

In 1939 Césaire postpones identifying his speaker. The first twenty-four strophes are a panoramic presentation of the island—poor, diseased, lacking a real identity—in which personification allows the hills (*mornes*), the shacks, and the unsanitary conditions of the little towns that grew up around the sugar plantations to express the physical degradation and the moral ugliness resulting from three centuries of colonial neglect. The population is present in the aggregate, an undifferentiated "one" or "you" that is then disarticulated into body parts—mouths, hands, feet, buttocks, genitals—in the Christmas festivity section. Punctuation is typical of parataxis: commas, semicolons, colons, which serve to pile up effects until they overwhelm the reader's senses (Edwards 2005, Kouassi 2006). The "I" emerges only in strophe 25, where Césaire focuses on a foul-smelling shack as a synecdoche of colonial society. Introduction of the speaker's family at this point stresses the mother's sacrifice for her children and the father's moods alternating between "melancholy tenderness" and "towering flames of anger." The transition from the first to the second sequence involves a shift of focus away from the sickness of colonial society to the speaker's own delusions. He alludes in strophe 29 to "betrayed trusts" and "uncertain evasive duty." He imagines his own heroic return to the island: "I would arrive sleek and young in this land of mine and I would say to this land . . ." In the course of the second sequence the speaker comes very gradually to a realization of his own alienation as a consequence of colonial education. Moral prostration and a diminished sense of self are related directly to the colonial process and its cultural institutions. The same strophe includes the long narrative segment devoted to the old black man on the streetcar. Césaire multiplies signifiers of blackness that clearly denote both his physical and moral self. Centuries of dehumanization have produced a "masterpiece of caricature." Structural symmetry in the 1939 "Notebook" is important here. The streetcar scene in the second sequence calls to mind the scene representing the speaker's family shack in the initial sequence. Both serve to bring a sharper focus to their respective themes: first physical, then moral degradation.

The third sequence introduces a series of interrogations about the meaning of blackness or negritude in the context of the speaker's alienation from those values he will posit as African. From this point onward the speaker adopts a prayerful attitude that is signaled formally by ritual language: "O" (twice in strophe 64) and "Eia" (twice in strophe 66). Numerous commentators have located "Eia" in Greek tragedy, but it occurs in the Latin missal as well. In both instances these are formal devices that lend gravity to the litany of characteristics Césaire enumerates in strophes 64–66 by means of the anaphora "those who" (7 times), "my Negritude" (3 times), "it takes root / breaks through" (3 times, further extending the litany of "my Negritude"). These three strophes and the one that follows immediately (67) afford a positive response to the negative characteristics of colonized peoples in strophe 61. In this new sequence Césaire evokes the "Ethiopian" peoples of Africa, whose fundamental difference from Hamitic peoples he learned from Leo Frobenius's book on African civilization. Suzanne Césaire described these traits in *Tropiques*:

> Ethiopian civilization is tied to the plant, to the vegetative cycle. // It is dreamlike, mystical and turned inward. The Ethiopian does not seek to understand phenomena, to seize and dominate exterior reality. It gives itself over to living a life identical to that of the plant, confident in life's continuity: germinate, grow, flower, fruit, and the cycle begins again (S. Césaire 1941).

In the third sequence Césaire sets up a contrapuntal structure in which the Ethiopian characteristics of sub-Saharan Africans, as the Césaires understood them, are set over against a Splengerian evocation of European decadence in strophes 39 and 70. This structure brings about a reversal of attitude on the part of the speaker, who in strophe 61 could see only the negative connotations of these same characteristics. The beginning of his own personal transformation shows him that these peoples are "truly the eldest sons of the world" and, indeed, the "flesh of the world's flesh pulsating with the very motion of the world."

A dozen strophes, from 80 to 91, detail the sufferings of African slaves ripped from their home cultures to toil, suffer, and die in the plantations of the Americas from Brazil through the West Indies to the southern United States. Names of diseases are enumerated like rosary beads, in strophe 87, before the speaker intones a litany of the punishments permitted by the Black Code that governed slaves' lives until abolition in 1848. The network of religious allusion in which his denunciation of slavery is couched has gone largely unnoticed. Kesteloot, in a monograph intended for student readers of the poem, saw in "I accept . . . I accept . . . totally, without reservation . . ." a textual allusion to Christ on the cross speaking to God the Father (Luke 22:42). In the phrase "Look, now I am only a man . . ." she heard a satirical echo of Pontius Pilate giving Jesus over to rabbinical judgment (John 19:5). Whether or not one accepts these specific interpretations, the phrase "my race that no ablution of hyssop mixed with lilies could purify" clearly recalls the text of Psalm 51:7. In "my race ripe grapes for drunken feet" Kesteloot heard an echo of Isaiah 63:3, and in "my queen of spittle and leprosy . . ." one of Mathew 27:30 (Kesteloot 1983). What matters here is not the precise intertext but rather the spiritual tone of supplication and prayer by which the speaker takes upon himself the sins of the past and prepares to expiate them. His intention is messianic rather than specifically christic. To put it in terms of I. A. Richards's theory of metaphor, the vehicle here is biblical, but the tenor relates to spiritual renewal of the race (Richards 1936). It is probable that Césaire used this technique to give voice to Du Bois's double consciousness. His goal is to create for colonized blacks in the French empire a version of Alain Locke's New Negro. Like many modernists in the English-speaking world, he used the language of religion—or, more accurately, a comparative mythology that includes the Bible—to elaborate a vocabulary and syntax of spiritual renewal. In this sense, his relationship to Catholicism is an aspect of countermodernism (Walker 1999). As the penultimate sequence of the "Notebook" comes to its climax, the speaker prepares to undergo a profound transformation. Stanzas 88 and 89 present the geography of suffering black humanity, the latter strophe replying directly to the claims made by "scientific" racism in strophe 52 in the context of the speaker's assimilationist delirium. His infernal descent hits bottom in strophe 90: "and the Negro every day more base, more cowardly, more sterile, less profound, more spilled out of himself, more separated from himself, more wily with himself, less immediate to himself." The isolated line that constitutes strophe 91 reiterates the spiritual motif of sacrifice: "I accept, I accept it all." This is the goal of the process of anagnorisis. With self-awareness comes a new knowledge of what is at stake. The speaker must, in conclusion, reach a position that transcends the colonial deadend.

The speaker's spiritual renewal opens with a pietà. The body of his country, its bones broken, is placed in his despairing arms. In strophe 92 the life force overwhelms him like some cosmic bull that lends its regenerative power. The initially bizarre image of the speaker spilling his seed upon the ground like the biblical Onan invites the reader to consider a far more primitive scene of the fecund earth being impregnated by the speaker's sperm. The round shape of the *mornes*, which early on had assumed a symbolic role in the geography of the island, now becomes the breast whose nipple is surrounded by a new life-giving force. The entire island becomes a living, sexualized being that responds to the speaker's firm embrace. Cyclones are its great breath, and volcanoes contain the seismic pulse of this mother goddess with whom the speaker breaks the taboo of incest. The consequences of this life-giving embrace are immediate and profoundly transformative. Already in strophe 93 the island is standing erect, side by side with her lover-son who through strophe 96 will denounce the centuries-old process of pseudomorphosis.

A parenthesis is in order here. Pseudomorphosis was readily identifiable in 1939 as a key word in the lexicon of Oswald Spengler, whose *Decline of the West* was much discussed between the two world wars. After 1945 Spengler was denounced as a forerunner of Nazi ideology and quickly forgotten. To our knowledge no critic of Césaire has ever seen its crucial function in the "Notebook." By including this technical term toward the end of the third sequence of his long poem, Césaire named the process by which the speaker and his island society had come to be physically ill, morally prostrate, and ideologically deluded. In Césaire's view colonial society had been impeded from developing its own original forms and institutions by the imposition of French cultural norms on a population transported from Africa. *Négritude* as it is presented in the poem did not yet exist in 1939, still less was it the harbinger of any movement, as readers of the post-1956 text would have it. *Négritude* is posited in the poem as the ideal result of a dramatic transformative process that must overthrow the old behaviors (*la vieille négritude*) so that a new black humanity (negritude in its positive sense) could emerge.

Consequently the meanings attaching to *nègre* and its compounds in the "Notebook" run the gamut from extremely negative to supremely positive. To render meaningfully the dialectical process that the speaker undergoes in the third and fourth sequences of the poem we have had to use words that are not acceptable today in civil discourse in English.

Césaire will finally exorcise the memory of the slave ship in strophes 103–105. He first announces its death throes: "The ghastly tapeworm of its cargo gnaws the fetid guts of the strange suckling of the sea!" He then details the horrors inflicted upon slaves carried on ships surprised on the high seas after the abolition of the trade. The images of horizontality that signaled the sick colonial society at the beginning of the poem are abruptly countered by a new vertical imagery. The adverb "debout" is repeated seventeen times in strophes 107–108. We shall never know what the original conclusion of the poem was. The sole surviving edited type-script is accompanied by a manuscript conclusion that begins with the last five lines of strophe 108. In an accompanying letter to the editor of *Volontés*, Césaire called his new ending "more conclusive" than the one he had originally submitted for publication.[2] In the penultimate strophe the speaker identifies with the *mauvais nègre* who calls all of nature into play during his transformation. He enjoins the spirit of the air to take over from an unreliable sun: "encoil yourself," "devour," "embrace," and especially "bind me." The images of binding by the wind (7 repetitions) complete the series begun by "devour" and "encoil." The speaker is to be bound to his people in a sacrificial act that sanctifies the transition from individual to collective identity. If the reader has followed the multiple biblical allusions that have sustained the vehicle of this transformation, it becomes clear in the final dramatic strophe that the Holy Spirit of Christianity has been supplanted by an ancient divinity resident in the natural world. This is particularly apparent in the final image of a celestial Dove that, after ritually strangling the speaker with its lasso of stars, bears him up to the heavens. After expressing an earlier desire to drown himself in despair, the speaker utters a final sybilline phrase that brings the poem to its abrupt conclusion: "It is there I will now fish / the malevolent tongue of the night in its still verticity!"

Since 1956 readers of Aimé Césaire's long poem have had to wrestle with what is, in effect, a palimpsest. On three occasions after the pre-original publication in *Volontés*, on the eve of World War II, Césaire over-wrote the carefully composed poem in a new spirit and with different aims. From 1939 to 1947 Césaire reinforced the existing structure of the 1939 text at its nodal points. In January 1947 the Paris bookseller Brentano's, who published in New York City during the war, brought out the original French-language edition of the *Cahier* with an English translation by L. Abel and Y. Goll. André Breton's preface "A Great Negro Poet" was first printed in Goll's New York magazine *Hémisphères* in autumn 1943, then reprinted in *Tropiques* the following year. A footnote to the *Tropiques* printing announced the imminent publication of Césaire's poem in New York (Breton 1944). The three-year delay in publication has been the source of considerable confusion. Moreover, the New York edition never circulated in Paris and was long thought to be identical to one published in Paris by Bordas a few weeks later. Breton's "A Great Negro Poet" also prefaced the Bordas edition, which reinforced the false assumption of identical texts. Césaire had in fact prepared the Paris edition from a different typescript (no longer extant) that he probably worked on in 1946 as his first poetry collection *Les Armes miraculeuses* (*The Miraculous Weapons*) neared publication. Although the Paris text shares the principal characteristics of surrealist metaphor with the New York original edition, it differs significantly from it. With respect to the 1939 text Césaire proceeded in 1947 by accretion, adding new elements to heighten certain effects. At strophe 29, just as the poem is about to move into the second sequence, Césaire added a new block of text, four strophes in the Brentano's edition and two in the Bordas that are substantially identical except for the stanza breaks. (The sense of choppiness created by division into shorter strophes is a general characteristic of the Brentano's edition, which Césaire probably did not see prior to publication.) These additions are a clear indicator of Césaire's desire to reinforce the sense of transition and modulation at two more strategic points in the poem, both of which follow an isolated alexandrine line. It is clear from his work on the Bordas edition that Césaire continued to work on the architectonics of the 1939 "Notebook" well into 1947.[3]

In October 1943, after revising the *Volontés* text of the "Notebook," Césaire wrote in *Tropiques* that to "Maintain Poetry" one had to: "defend oneself against social concerns by creating a zone of incandescence, on the near side of which, within which there flowers in terrible security the unheard blossom of the "I"; to strip all material existence in silence and in the high glacial fires of humor; whether by the creation of a zone of fire or by the creation of a zone of frozen silence; to conquer through revolt the free part where one may summon one's self intact, such are the exigencies which for the past century have guided every poet" (Césaire 1943b). This statement of poetic purpose harmonizes perfectly with the essay on Lautréamont that Césaire had published in February 1943: "By way of the image one goes toward the infinite. Lautréamont established this as a definitive truth" (Césaire 1943a). The Brentano's text, completed when the outcome of World War II was still in doubt, became the most searingly surrealist version of Césaire's poem.

During the four succeeding years Césaire was elected mayor of Fort-de-France and Communist Deputy from Central Martinique to the constituent assembly of the Fourth Republic. He co-sponsored the 1946 law that transformed his native land legally from a colony to an overseas département of France. As mayor of Fort-de-France he found himself dealing with the most troublesome infrastructure problems of the run-down colonial capital he had described in such disgusting terms a decade earlier. At home he struggled with the central government's reluctance to honor its commitments to the new département, while it introduced a new level of French-born administrators who brought with them prejudices alien to creole society. In the Chamber of Deputies he soon found himself and his colleagues on the left overwhelmed by the Gaullist majority who would do no more than was absolutely necessary to improve conditions in the former colonies. As a member of an anti-capitalist political party that had criticized the surrealist style of his first collection of poetry, *The Miraculous Weapons*, in 1946, he found himself duty-bound to introduce in 1947 the social issues he had eschewed in 1943. These constraints brought about one further, and major, modification of the text of the Bordas edition of the *Notebook*. For the first time, the poem is framed by a new initial strophe that is counterbalanced by four short strophes introduced between 108 and 109. Few readers of the *Notebook* realize that the powerful strophe beginning "Beat it, I said to him, you cop, you lousy pig, beat it. I detest the flunkies of order . . ." (Césaire 1983) did not exist prior to the first Paris edition of the poem. Who is this "I" who denounces a repressive social order? Where does he come from? The interjection of this strong first-person political statement in the initial strophe of this and all subsequent versions unbalances the equilibrium so carefully established in 1939 between the anonymous throng in the first sequence and the eventual emergence of a first-person subject in the twenty-fifth strophe. New political allusions deflect the reader's attention away from the intensely subjective character of the speaker's transformation in the "Notebook." The four strophes that complete this new framing device likewise mask the spiritual nature of the speaker's quest by orienting our reading toward a quite different context. They slow down the original rapidity of the conclusion and set up constraints on meaning, effectively blocking the quest narrative that had carried the poem forward from 1939 to the Brentano's edition early in 1947.

Whereas the two 1947 editions were revised exclusively by the addition of new material to the 1939 preoriginal, inflecting and intensifying its effects, the 1956 edition excised much of that same material and substituted for it blocks of text that would align the poem with Césaire's new political position, which embraced the immediate decolonization of Africa in militant tones. Most notably the visible traces of a spiritual discourse were obliterated: a "catholic love" in 1939 became "love" in the New York edition, then a "tyrannical love" in the Bordas text. Onan disappeared altogether, along with the most obvious markers of the spiritual network of metaphors. The sexual metaphors that characterized the most carnal passages depicting the speaker's union with nature were replaced by new material that emphasized the appalling condition of humble laborers. A critical examination of these extensive cuts reveals the underlying purpose of Césaire's new approach (Arnold 2008). He removed nearly all the spiritual connotations (apocalypse, last judgment), attenuated the racialist discourse as well as several strophes that were self-consciously absurdist, and the majority of the passages marked by free associative metaphor (markers of surrealism). Substantial additions near the end of the third sequence introduced an entirely new socialist perspective focused on the wretched of the earth. Three new strophes named individual laborers who were sacrificed to the machinery of cane production in Martinique, thus leading the reader away from the spiritual sacrifice of the speaker and toward a sense of collective socialist action. The result is decisive; from 1956 onward the reader is no longer oriented toward a network of metaphors that undergird a drama of personal sacrifice. Henceforth the drama is a sociopolitical one that calls for decolonization and the democratization of economic institutions.

Serious readers of this poem have for decades struggled with the palimpsest effect of these multiple rewritings. In the 1980s we concluded that the *Cahier* resulted in the myth of the birth of the hero of Negritude (Arnold 1981) or "a parthenogenesis in which Césaire must conceive and give birth to himself while exorcising his introjected and collective white image of the black" (Eshleman 1983). Kesteloot had earlier read the final movement as "participating in the creative power of the Cosmos," and in a footnote she suggested a rite of possession that is "indispensable to African ceremonies and to Vodun in particular" (Kesteloot 1963). Condé, commenting on the same passage, wrote that "it's a miracle in the strictest sense that we are dealing with here, a transformation born of Faith that Reason could not account for" (Condé 1978). Others have gone in a distinctly cosmogonic direction (Pestre de Almeida 2010) or have embraced an esoteric mysticism (Paviot 2009). Fonkoua, on the other hand, has attended exclusively to the political overtones that were added belatedly (Fonkoua 2008).

Our intention in offering the 1939 French text of the "Notebook," translated for the first time into English, is to strip away decades of rewriting that introduced an ideological purpose absent from the original. We do not claim to reveal what the poem ultimately means but rather how it was meant to be read in 1939. Reading with the poem's first audience, so to speak, will finally permit a new generation to judge its enduring power a century after the poet's birth.

Notes

1. The alexandrine is a twelve-syllable line with a major division or caesura in the middle. On either side of the caesura two further rhythmic divisions are freer in form, varying from 3/3 to 5/1 (rare) with all the combinations in between at the disposal of the poet.

2. The edited typescript and the letter to the editor of *Volontés* can be consulted in the library of the French National Assembly. The letter is dated May 28, 1939.

3. This process will be much more apparent in the Paris edition of Césaire's *Poésie, Théâtre, Essais*, scheduled for publication in the Planète Libre collection at CNRS-Éditions. The four historic editions of the poem will be printed sequentially with annotations.

Works Cited

Arnold, A. James. *Modernism and Negritude: The Poetry and Poetics of Aimé Césaire.* Cambridge: Harvard University Press, 1981. 318 pages.

———. "Beyond Postcolonial Césaire: Reading *Cahier d'un retour au pays natal* Historically." *Forum for Modern Language Studies* 44, no.3 (2008): 258–75. (Pages 272–75 present a table of deleted material organized by type: spiritual, sexual, racial.)

Breton, André. "Martinique charmeuse de serpents: Un grand poète noir." *Tropiques* 11 (May 1944): 119–26. (A footnote assures readers that this text would preface the bilingual edition of the *Cahier*, which was to be published imminently by Hémisphères in New York. An announcement on page 98 of *VVV*, no. 4 [1944], published in New York, confirms this claim. In 1947 Breton's preface accompanied both the Brentano's and the Bordas editions of Césaire's poem.)

Césaire, Aimé. "Cahier d'un retour au pays natal," *Volontés*, no. 20 (August 1939): 23–51.

———. "En guise de manifeste littéraire." *Tropiques*, no. 5 (April 1942): 7–12.

———. 1943a. "Isidore Ducasse, comte de Lautréamont." *Tropiques*, nos. 6–7 (April 1943): 10–15.

———. 1943b. "Maintenir la poésie." *Tropiques*, nos. 8–9 (October 1943): 7–8.

———. 1947a. *Cahier d'un retour au pays natal / Memorandum on My Martinique*. Translated by Lionel Abel and Yvan Goll. Preface by André Breton. New York: Brentano's, 1947. 145 pages. (The English text followed the French. The precise date of publication was January 7, 1947.)

———. 1947b. *Cahier d'un retour au pays natal*. Preface by André Breton. Frontispiece by Wifredo Lam. Paris: Bordas, 1947. (The text of the poem runs from page 25 to page 96.)

———. *Cahier d'un retour au pays natal*. Paris: Présence Africaine, 1956. Preface by Petar Guberina. (The text of the poem can be found on pages 25–91. Substituting a preface by a professional linguist in a Yugoslav university for André Breton's removed the surrealist label from the poem and oriented it toward nonaligned socialism.)

———. *Poésie*. Vol. 1 of *Oeuvres complètes*. Paris and Fort-de-France: Désormeaux, 1976. 325 pages.

———. *The Collected Poetry*. Translated by Clayton Eshleman and Annette Smith. Berkeley and Los Angeles: University of California Press, 1983.

———. "Poetry and Knowledge." Translated by A. James Arnold, xlii–lvi. In *Lyric and Dramatic Poetry (1946–82)*. Translated by Clayton Eshleman and Annette Smith. CARAF Books. Charlottesville and London: University Press of Virginia, 1990.

———. *La Poésie*. Edited by D. Maximinin and G. Carpentier. Paris: Seuil, 1994. 550 pages.

———. *Solar Throat Slashed / Soleil cou coupé*. Translated and edited by A. James Arnold and Clayton Eshleman. Middletown, Conn.: Wesleyan University Press, 2011. 183 pages.

Césaire, Suzanne. "Léo Frobenius et le problème des civilisations." *Tropiques* 1 (April 1941): 27–36. (She underlined the link between Frobenius and the "Notebook" by ending her article on a quotation from her husband's 1939 poem.)

Condé, Maryse. *Césaire: Cahier d'un retour au pays natal*. Profil d'une oeuvre. Paris: Hatier, 1978.

Du Bois, W. E. B. *The Souls of Black Folk: Essays and Sketches*. Chicago: McClurg, 1903. 264 pages. (First French edition, Paris: Présence Africaine, 1959.)

Edwards, Brent Hayes. "Aimé Césaire and the Syntax of Influence." *Research in African Literatures* 36, no. 2 (2005): 1–18.

Eshleman, Clayton. "The Collections." In *Aimé Césaire: The Collected Poetry*. Berkeley and Los Angeles: University of California Press, 1983.

Fonkoua, Romuald. *Aimé Césaire*. Paris: Perrin, 2008. 392 pages. (Fonkoua minimized the role of Breton and the surrealists in the *Notebook*. Taking the post-1956 texts as the norm, he concluded that "if Césaire's poetics and style are free of any and all surrealist influence, it is quite simply due to the fact that surrealism had no attraction for the students preparing for the École Normale Supérieure between the two world wars" (62). Clearly the rewriting of the 1956 *Cahier* had achieved its goal. For this critic and many others the palimpsest was perfectly invisible.)

Kesteloot, Lilyan. *Les Écrivains noirs de langue française: Naissance d'une littérature*. Brussels: Disputats, 1963. (Reprinted in 1963 by the Solvay Institute of Sociology of the Free University of Brussels. Arguably the most influential reading of the *Cahier / Notebook* as a political poem.)

————. *Comprendre le* Cahier d'un retour au pays natal *d'Aimé Césaire*. Versailles: Les Classiques Africains, 1983. 127 pages. (Reprinted in 1990, it includes a brief glossary.)

Kouassi, Germain. *La Poésie de Césaire par la langue et le style: l'exemple du* "Cahier d'un retour au pays natal." Paris: Publibook, 2006. 134 pages.

Ngal, Georges (M.aM.) *Aimé Césaire: Un homme à la recherche d'une patrie*. Dakar and Abidjan: Nouvelles Éditions Africaines, 1975. 293 pages. (In 1994 Présence Africaine brought out a reprint edition.)

Paviot, Christian. *Césaire autrement: Le mysticisme du* Cahier d'un retour au pays natal. Paris: L'Harmattan, 2009. 79 pages. (Egyptian mythology, Old Testament allusions and tarot cards enter into this esoteric reading of the poem.)

Pestre de Almeida, Lilian. *Mémoire et métamorphose: Aimé Césaire entre l'oral et l'écrit*. Würzburg: Königshausen & Neumann, 2010. 433 pages. (The first chapter is devoted to a careful and extended analysis of the Brentano's edition, which the author considers an anomaly. Her teleological approach sees the rewriting from the Bordas (1947) to the Présence Africaine (1956) edition as the norm.)

Walker, Keith L. *Countermodernism and Francophone Literary Culture: The Game of Slipknot*. New Americanists. Durham, N.C.: Duke University Press, 1999. 301 pages.

The Original 1939
Notebook of a Return to the Native Land

CAHIER D'UN RETOUR AU PAYS NATAL

[1]

Au bout du petit matin bourgeonnant d'anses frêles les Antilles qui ont faim, les Antilles grêlées de petite vérole, les Antilles dynamitées d'alcool, échouées dans la boue de cette baie, dans la poussière de cette ville sinistrement échouées.

[2]

Au bout du petit matin, l'extrême, trompeuse désolée eschare sur la blessure des eaux ; les martyrs qui ne témoignent pas ; les fleurs du sang qui se fanent et s'éparpillent dans le vent inutile comme des cris de perroquets babillards ; une vieille vie menteusement souriante, ses lèvres ouvertes d'angoisses désaffectées ; une vieille misère pourrissant sous le soleil, silencieusement ; un vieux silence crevant de pustules tièdes

[3]

l'affreuse inanité de notre raison d'être.

[4]

Au bout du petit matin, sur cette plus fragile épaisseur de terre que dépasse de façon humiliante son grandiose avenir—les volcans éclateront, l'eau nue emportera les taches mûres du soleil et il ne restera plus qu'un bouillonnement tiède picoré d'oiseaux marins—la plage des songes et l'insensé réveil.

[5]

Au bout du petit matin, cette ville plate—étalée, trébuchée de son bon sens, inerte, essoufflée sous son fardeau géométrique de croix éternellement recommençante, indocile à son sort, muette, contrariée de toutes façons, incapable de croître selon le suc de cette terre, embarrassée, rognée, réduite, en rupture de faune et de flore.

[6]

Au bout du petit matin, cette ville plate—étalée. . .

Et dans cette ville inerte, cette foule criarde si étonnamment passée à côté de son cri comme cette ville à côté de son mouvement, de son sens,

[1]

At the end of first light burgeoning with frail coves the hungry Antilles, the Antilles pitted with smallpox, the Antilles dynamited by alcohol, stranded in the mud of this bay, in the dust of this town sinisterly stranded.

[2]

At the end of first light, the extreme, deceptive desolate eschar on the wound of the waters; the martyrs who do not bear witness; the flowers of blood that fade and scatter in the empty wind like the cries of babbling parrots; an aged life mendaciously smiling, its lips opened by vacated agonies; an aged poverty rotting under the sun, silently; an aged silence bursting with tepid pustules

[3]

the dreadful inanity of our raison d'être.

[4]

At the end of first light, on this very fragile earth thickness exceeded in a humiliating way by its grandiose future—the volcanoes will explode,* the naked water will bear away the ripe sun stains and nothing will be left but a tepid bubbling pecked at by sea birds—the beach of dreams and the insane awakening.

[5]

At the end of first light, this town sprawled—flat, toppled from its common sense, inert, winded under its geometric weight of an eternally renewed cross, indocile to its fate, mute, vexed no matter what, incapable of growing according to the juice of this earth, encumbered, clipped, reduced, in breach of its fauna and flora.

[6]

At the end of first light, this town sprawled—flat. . . .
And in this inert town, this squalling throng so astonishingly detoured from its cry like this town from its movement, from its meaning, not even

sans inquiétude, à côté de son vrai cri, le seul qu'on eût voulu l'entendre crier parce qu'on le sent sien lui seul ; parce qu'on le sent habiter en elle dans quelque refuge profond d'ombre et d'orgueil, dans cette ville inerte, cette foule à côté de son cri de faim, de misère, de révolte, de haine, cette foule si étrangement bavarde et muette.

[7]

Dans cette ville inerte, cette étrange foule qui ne s'entasse pas, ne se mêle pas ; habile à découvrir le point de désencastration, de fuite, d'esquive. Cette foule qui ne sait pas faire foule, cette foule, on s'en rend compte, si parfaitement seule sous ce soleil, à la façon dont une femme, toute on eût cru à la cadence lyrique de ses fesses, interpelle brusquement une pluie hypothétique et lui intime l'ordre de ne pas tomber ; ou à un signe rapide de croix sans mobile visible ; ou à l'animalité subitement grave d'une paysanne, urinant debout, les jambes écartées, roides.

[8]

Dans cette ville inerte, cette foule désolée sous le soleil, ne participant à rien de ce qui s'exprime, s'affirme, se libère au grand jour de cette terre sienne. Ni à l'Impératrice Joséphine des Français rêvant très haut au dessus de la négraille. Ni au libérateur figé dans sa libération de pierre blanchie. Ni au conquistador. Ni à ce mépris, ni à cette liberté, ni à cette audace.

[9]

Au bout du petit matin, cette ville inerte et ses au-delà de lèpres, de consomption, de famines, de peurs tapies dans les ravins, de peurs juchées dans les arbres, de peurs creusées dans le sol, de peurs en dérive dans le ciel, de peurs amoncelées et ses fumerolles d'angoisse.

[10]

Au bout du petit matin le morne oublié, oublieux de sauter.

[11]

Au bout du petit matin le morne au sabot inquiet et docile—son sang impaludé met en déroute le soleil de ses pouls surchauffés.

worried, detoured from its true cry, the only cry one would have wanted to hear because it alone feels at home in this town; because one feels that it inhabits some deep refuge of shadow and of pride, in this inert town, this throng detoured from its cry of hunger, of poverty, of revolt, of hatred, this throng so strangely chattering and mute.

[7]

In this inert town, this strange throng that does not huddle, does not mix; clever at discovering the point of disencasement, of flight, of dodging. This throng that does not know how to throng, this throng, one realizes, so perfectly alone under the sun, like a woman one thought completely occupied with the lyric cadence of her buttocks, who abruptly challenges a hypothetical rain and enjoins it not to fall; or like a rapid sign of the cross without perceptible motive; or like the sudden grave animality of a peasant, urinating standing, her legs parted, stiff.

[8]

In this inert town, this desolate throng under the sun, not connected with anything that is expressed, asserted, released in broad earth daylight, its own. Not with Josephine, Empress of the French, dreaming way up there above the nigger scum. Nor with the liberator fixed in his whitewashed stone liberation. Nor with the conquistador.* Nor with this contempt, nor with this freedom, nor with this audacity.

[9]

At the end of first light, this inert town and its beyond of lepers, of consumption, of famines, of fears crouched in the ravines, of fears perched in the trees, of fears dug in the ground, of fears adrift in the sky, of piled up fears and their fumaroles of anguish.

[10]

At the end of first light the morne* forgotten, forgetful of exploding.

[11]

At the end of first light the morne in restless, docile hooves—its malarial blood routs the sun with its overheated pulse.

5

[12]

Au bout du petit matin l'incendie contenu du morne, comme un san-
glot que l'on a bâillonné au bord de son éclatement sanguinaire, en quête
d'une ignition qui se dérobe et se méconnaît.

[13]

Au bout du petit matin, le morne accroupi devant la boulimie aux aguets
de foudres et de moulins, lentement vomissant ses fatigues d'hommes, le
morne seul et son sang répandu, le morne et ses pansements d'ombre, le
morne et ses rigoles de peur, le morne et ses grandes mains de vent.

[14]

Au bout du petit matin, le morne famélique et nul ne sait mieux que
ce morne bâtard pourquoi le suicide s'est étouffé avec complicité de son
hypoglosse en retournant sa langue pour l'avaler ; pourquoi une femme
semble faire la planche à la rivière Capot (son corps lumineusement
obscur s'organise docilement au commandement du nombril) mais elle
n'est qu'un paquet d'eau sonore.

[15]

Et ni l'instituteur dans sa classe, ni le prêtre au catéchisme ne pourront
tirer un mot de ce négrillon somnolent, malgré leur manière si énergique
à tous deux de tambouriner son crâne tondu, car c'est dans les marais de
la faim que s'est enlisée sa voix d'inanition (un mot-un-seul-mot et je-
vous-en-tiens-quitte-de-la-reine-Blanche-de-Castille, un mot-un-seul-mot,
voyez-vous-ce-petit-sauvage-qui-ne-sait-pas-un-seul-des-dix-commande-
ments-de-Dieu),
    car sa voix s'oublie dans les marais de la faim,
    et il n'y a rien, rien à tirer vraiment de ce petit vaurien,
    qu'une faim qui ne sait plus grimper aux agrès de sa voix,
    une faim lourde et veule,
    une faim ensevelie au plus profond de la Faim de ce morne famélique.

[16]

Au bout du petit matin, l'échouage hétéroclite, les puanteurs exacerbées
de la corruption, les sodomies monstrueuses de l'hostie et du victimaire,
les coltis infranchissables du préjugé et de la sottise, les prostitutions,
les hypocrisies, les lubricités, les trahisons, les mensonges, les faux, les

At the end of first light the restrained conflagration of the morne, like a sob gagged on the verge of a bloodthirsty burst, in quest of an ignition that slips away and ignores itself.

At the end of first light, the morne crouching before bulimia on the outlook for tuns and mills, slowly vomiting out its human fatigue, the morne solitary and its blood shed, the morne bandaged in shade, the morne and its ditches of fear, the morne and its great hands of wind.

At the end of first light, the famished morne and no one knows better than this bastard morne why the suicide* choked with a little help from his hypoglossal jamming his tongue backward to swallow it; why a woman seems to float belly up on the Capot River* (her chiaroscuro body submissively organized at the command of her navel) but she is only a bundle of sonorous water.

And neither the teacher in his classroom, nor the priest at catechism will be able to get a word out of this sleepy little picaninny, no matter how energetically they drum on his shorn skull, for starvation has quicksanded his voice into the swamp of hunger (a word-one-single-word and we-will-forget-about-Queen-Blanche-of-Castille,* a word-one-single-word, you-should see-this-little-savage-who-doesn't-know-any-of-God's-Ten-Commandments),
   for his voice gets lost in the swamp of hunger,
   and there is nothing, really nothing to squeeze out of this little brat,
   other than a hunger that can no longer climb to the rigging of his voice,
   a sluggish flabby hunger,
   a hunger buried in the depths of the Hunger of this famished morne.

At the end of first light, the disparate stranding, the exacerbated stench of corruption, the monstrous sodomies of the host and the sacrificing priest, the impassable beakhead frames of prejudice and stupidity, the prostitutions, the hypocrisies, the lubricities, the treasons, the lies, the

concussions—l'essoufflement des lâchetés insuffisantes, l'enthousiasme sans ahan aux poussis surnuméraires, les avidités, les hystéries, les perversions, les arlequinades de la misère, les estropiements, les prurits, les urticaires, les hamacs tièdes de la dégénérescence. Ici la parade des risibles et scrofuleux bubons, les poutures de microbes très étranges, les poisons sans alexitère connu, les sanies de plaies bien antiques, les fermentations imprévisibles d'espèces putrescibles.

[17]

Au bout du petit matin, la grande nuit immobile, les étoiles plus mortes qu'un balafong crevé.

[18]

Le bulbe tératique de la nuit, germé de nos bassesses et de nos renoncements. . .

[19]

Et nos gestes imbéciles et fous pour faire revivre l'éclaboussement d'or des instants favorisés, le cordon ombilical restitué à sa splendeur fragile, le pain, et le vin de la complicité, le pain, le vin, le sang des épousailles véridiques.

[20]

Et cette joie ancienne m'apportant la connaissance de ma présente misère,
une route bossuée qui pique une tête dans un creux où elle éparpille quelques cases ; une route infatigable qui charge à fond de train un morne en haut duquel elle s'enlise brutalement dans une mare de maisons pataudes, une route follement montante, témérairement descendante, et la carcasse de bois comiquement juchée sur de minuscules pattes de ciment que j'appelle « notre maison », sa coiffure de tôle ondulant au soleil comme une peau qui sèche, la salle à manger, le plancher grossier où luisent des têtes de clous, les solives de sapin et d'ombre qui courent au plafond, les chaises de paille fantômales, la lumière grise de la lampe, celle vernissée et rapide des cancrelats qui bourdonne à faire mal. . .

frauds, the concussions—the panting of a deficient cowardice, the heave-holess enthusiasm of supernumerary sahibs, the greeds, the hysterias, the perversions, the harlequinades of poverty, the cripplings, the pruritus, the urticaria, the tepid hammocks of degeneracy. Right here the parade of laughable and scrofulous buboes, the forced feeding of very strange microbes, the poisons without known alexins, the sanies of really ancient sores, the unforeseeable fermentations of putrescible species.

[17]

At the end of first light, the great still night, the stars deader than a smashed balafo.

[18]

The teratical bulb of night, sprouted from our villainies and our self-denials . . .

[19]

And our idiotic and insane stunts to revive the golden splashing of privileged moments, the umbilical cord restored to its ephemeral splendor, the bread, and the wine of complicity, the bread, the wine, the blood of veracious weddings.

[20]

And this joy of former times making me aware of my present poverty, a bumpy road plunging into a hollow where it scatters a few shacks; an indefatigable road charging at full speed a morne at the top of which it brutally quicksands into a pool of clumsy houses, a road foolishly climbing, recklessly descending, and the carcass of wood, which I call "our house," comically perched on minute cement paws, its coiffure of corrugated iron in the sun like a skin laid out to dry, the dining room, the rough floor where nail heads gleam, the beams of pine and shadow across the ceiling, the spectral straw chairs, the gray lamp light, the glossy flash of cockroaches in a maddening buzz . . .

Au bout du petit matin, ce plus essentiel pays restitué à ma gourmandise, non de diffuse tendresse, mais la tourmentée concentration sensuelle du gras téton des mornes avec l'accidentel palmier comme son germe durci, la jouissance saccadée des torrents et depuis Trinité jusqu'à Grand-Rivière, la grand'lèche hystérique de la mer.

Et le temps passait vite, très vite.

Passés août où les manguiers pavoisent de toutes leurs lunules, septembre l'accoucheur de cyclônes, octobre le flambeur de cannes, novembre qui ronronne aux distilleries, c'était Noël qui commençait.

Il s'était annoncé d'abord Noël par un picotement de désirs, une soif de tendresses neuves, un bourgeonnement de rêves imprécis, puis il s'était envolé tout à coup dans le froufrou violet de ses grandes ailes de joie, et alors c'était parmi le bourg sa vertigineuse retombée qui éclatait la vie des cases comme une grenade trop mûre.

Noël n'était pas comme toutes les fêtes. Il n'aimait pas à courir les rues, à danser sur les places publiques, à s'installer sur les chevaux de bois, à profiter de la cohue pour pincer les femmes, à lancer des feux d'artifice au front des tamariniers. Il avait l'agoraphobie, Noël. Ce qu'il lui fallait c'était toute une journée d'affairement, d'apprêts, de cuisinages, de nettoyages, d'inquiétudes, de peur-que-ça
ne-suffise-pas,
de-peur-que-ça-ne-manque,
de-peur-qu'on-ne-s'embête,
puis le soir une petite église pas intimidante qui se laissât emplir bienveillamment par les rires, les chuchotis, les confidences, les déclarations amoureuses, les médisances et la cacophonie gutturale d'un chantre bien d'attaque et aussi de gais copains et de franches luronnes et des cases aux entrailles riches en succulences, et pas regardantes, et l'on s'y parque une vingtaine, et la rue est déserte, et le bourg n'est plus qu'un bouquet de chants, et l'on est bien à l'intérieur, et l'on en mange du bon, et l'on en boit du réjouissant et il y a du boudin, celui étroit de deux doigts qui s'enroule en volubile, celui large et trapu, le bénin à goût de serpolet, le violent à incandescence pimentée, et du café brûlant et de l'anis sucré, et du punch au lait, et le soleil liquide des rhums, et toutes sortes de

At the end of first light, this most essential land restored to my gour-mandize, not in diffuse tenderness, but the tormented sensual concentra-tion of the fat tits of the mornes with an occasional palm tree as their hardened sprout, the jerky orgasm of torrents and from Trinité to Grand-Rivière* the hysterical grandsuck of the sea.

And time passed quickly, very quickly.

After August and mango trees decked out in all their lunules, Septem-ber begetter of cyclones, October igniter of sugarcane, November purring in the distilleries, there came Christmas.

It had come in first, Christmas did, with a tingling of desires, a thirst for new tendernesses, a burgeoning of vague dreams, then with a purple rustle of its great joyous wings it had suddenly flown away, and after that its abrupt fall out over the village making shack life burst like an overripe pomegranate.

Christmas was not like other holidays. It didn't like to gad about the streets, to dance on public squares, to mount the carousel horses, to use the crowd to pinch women, to hurl fireworks into the faces of the tamarind trees. It had agoraphobia, Christmas did. What it wanted was a whole day of bustling, preparing, a cooking and cleaning spree, endless jitters, about
not-having-enough,
about-running-short,
about-getting-bored,
then at evening an unimposing little church that would benevolently make room for the laughter, the whispers, the secrets, the love talk, the gossip and the guttural cacophony of a plucky singer and also boister-ous pals and shameless hussies and shacks up to their guts in succulent goodies, and not stingy, and twenty people can crowd in, and the street is deserted, and the village turns into a bouquet of singing, and you are cozy in there, and you eat good, and you drink heartily, and there are blood sausages, one kind only two fingers wide twined in coils, another broad and stocky, the mild one tasting of wild thyme, the hot one spiced to an incandescence, and steaming coffee and sugared anisette, and milk

bonnes choses qui vous imposent autoritairement les muqueuses ou vous les fondent en subtilités, ou vous les distillent en ravissements, ou vous les tissent de fragrances, et l'on rit, et l'on chante, et les refrains fusent à perte de vue comme des cocotiers :

ALLELUIA

KYRIE ELEISON. . . LEISON. . . LEISON,

CHRISTE ELEISON. . . LEISON. . . LEISON.

Et ce ne sont pas seulement les bouches qui chantent, mais les mains, mais les pieds, mais les fesses, mais les sexes, et la créature tout entière qui se liquéfie en sons, voix et rythme.

Arrivée au sommet de son ascension, la joie crève comme un nuage. Les chants ne s'arrêtent pas, mais ils roulent maintenant inquiets et lourds par les vallées de la peur, les tunnels de l'angoisse et les feux de l'enfer.

Et chacun se met à tirer par la queue le diable le plus proche, jusqu'à ce que la peur s'abolisse insensiblement dans les fines sablures du rêve, et l'on vit comme dans un rêve véritablement, et l'on boit et l'on crie et l'on chante comme dans un rêve, et on somnole aussi comme dans un rêve avec des paupières en pétales de rose, et le jour vient velouté comme une sapotille, et l'odeur de purin des cacaoyers, et les dindons qui égrènent leurs pustules rouges au soleil, et l'obsession des cloches, et la pluie,

les cloches. . . la pluie. . .

qui tintent, tintent, tintent. . .

[23]

Au bout du petit matin, cette ville plate—étalée. . .

Elle rampe sur les mains sans jamais aucune envie de vriller le ciel d'une stature de protestation. Les dos des maisons ont peur du ciel truffé de feu, leurs pieds des noyades du sol, elles ont opté de se poser superficielles entre les surprises et les perfidies. Et pourtant elle avance la ville. Même qu'elle paît tous les jours plus outre sa marée de corridors carrelés, de persiennes pudibondes, de cours gluantes, de peintures qui dégoulinent. Et de petits scandales étouffés, de petites hontes tues, de petites haines immenses pétrissent en bosses et creux les rues étroites où le ruisseau grimace longitudinalement parmi l'étron. . .

[24]

Au bout du petit matin, la vie prostrée, on ne sait où dépêcher ses rêves avortés, le fleuve de vie désespérément torpide dans son lit, sans turges-

punch, and the liquid sun of rums, and all sorts of good things that drive your taste buds wild or dissolve them into subtleties, or distill them to the point of ecstacy or cocoon them with fragrances, and you laugh, and you sing, and the refrains flare on and on like coco palms:

ALLELUIA

KYRIE ELEISON . . . LEISON . . . LEISON,

CHRISTE ELEISON . . . LEISON . . . LEISON.

And not only do the mouths sing, but the hands, the feet, the buttocks, the genitals, and your entire being that liquefies into sounds, voices and rhythm.

At the peak of its ascent, joy bursts like a cloud. The songs don't stop, but roll now anxious and heavy through the valleys of fear, the tunnels of anguish and the fires of hell.

And everybody starts pulling the nearest devil by the tail, until fear imperceptibly fades in the fine sand lines of dream, and you really live as in a dream, and you drink and you shout and you sing as in a dream, and doze too as in a dream with rose petal eyelids, and the day comes velvety as a sapodilla, and the liquid manure smell of the cacao trees, and the turkeys shelling their red pustules in the sun, and the obsessive bells, and the rain,

the bells . . . the rain . . .

that tinkle, tinkle, tinkle . . .

[23]

At the end of first light, this town sprawled—flat . . .

It crawls on its hands without the slightest desire to drill the sky with a stature of protest. The backs of the houses are frightened by the sky truffled with fire, their feet by the drownings of the soil, they chose to perch shallowly between surprises and treacheries. And yet the town advances, yes it does. It even grazes every day further beyond its tide of tiled corridors, prudish shutters, gluey courtyards, dripping paintwork. And petty hushed-up scandals, petty unvoiced guilts, petty immense hatreds knead the narrow streets into bumps and potholes where the wastewater grins longitudinally through the turds . . .

[24]

At the end of first light, life prostrate, you don't know how to dispose of your aborted dreams, the river of life desperately torpid in its bed, neither

cence ni dépression, incertain de fluer, lamentablement vide, la lourde
impartialité de l'ennui, répartissant l'ombre sur toutes choses égales, l'air
stagnant sans une trouée d'oiseau clair.

[25]

Au bout du petit matin, une autre petite maison qui sent très mauvais
dans une rue très étroite, une maison minuscule qui abrite en ses entrailles
de bois pourri des dizaines de rats et la turbulence de mes six frères et
sœurs, une petite maison cruelle dont l'intransigeance affole nos fins de
mois et mon père fantasque grignoté d'une seule seule misère, je n'ai
jamais su laquelle, qu'une imprévisible sorcellerie assoupit en mélanco-
lique tendresse ou exalte en hautes flammes de colère ; et ma mère dont
les jambes pour notre faim inlassable pédalent, pédalent de jour, de nuit,
je suis même réveillé la nuit par ces jambes inlassables qui pédalent la
nuit et la morsure âpre dans la chair molle de la nuit d'une Singer que ma
mère pédale, pédale pour notre faim et de jour et de nuit.

[26]

Au bout du petit matin, au delà de mon père, de ma mère, la case
gerçant d'ampoules, comme un pêcher tourmenté de la cloque, et le toit
aminci, rapiécé de morceaux de bidon de pétrole, et ça fait des marais
de rouillure dans la pâte grise sordide empuantie de la paille, et quand
le vent siffle, ces disparates font bizarre le bruit, comme un crépitement
de friture d'abord, puis comme un tison que l'on plonge dans l'eau avec
la fumée des brindilles qui s'envole. . . Et le lit de planches d'où s'est
levée ma race, tout entière ma race de ce lit de planches, avec ses pattes
de caisses de Kérosine, comme s'il avait l'éléphantiasis le lit, et sa peau
de cabri, et ses feuilles de banane séchées, et ses haillons, une nostalgie
de matelas le lit de ma grand-mère (Au dessus du lit, dans un pot plein
d'huile un lumignon dont la flamme danse comme un gros ravet. . . sur le
pot en lettres d'or : merci).

[27]

Et une honte, cette rue Paille,
un appendice dégoûtant comme les parties honteuses du bourg qui étend
à droite et à gauche, tout au long de la route coloniale, la houle grise de
ses toits « d'essentes ». Ici il n'y a que des toits de paille que l'embrun a
brunis et que le vent épile.

turgid nor low, hesitant to flow, pitifully empty, the impartial heaviness of boredom distributing shade equally on all things, the stagnant air unbroken by the brightness of a single bird.

[25]

At the end of first light, another little house very bad-smelling in a very narrow street, a miniscule house that harbors in its guts of rotten wood dozens of rats and the turbulence of my six brothers and sisters, a cruel little house whose demands panic the ends of our months and my temperamental father gnawed by one persistent ache, I never knew which one, whom an unexpected sorcery could lull to melancholy tenderness or drive to towering flames of anger, and my mother whose legs pedal, pedal, day and night, for our tireless hunger, I am even awakened at night by these tireless legs pedaling by night and the bitter bite in the soft flesh of the night by a Singer that my mother pedals, pedals for our hunger both day and night.

[26]

At the end of first light, beyond my father, my mother, the shack chapped with blisters, like a peach tree afflicted with curl, and the thin roof patched with pieces of gasoline cans, which create swamps of rust in the stinking sordid gray straw pulp, and when the wind whistles, these odds and ends make a noise bizarre, first like the crackling of frying, then like a brand dropped into water the smoke of its twigs flying up . . . And the bed of boards from which my race arose, my whole entire race from this bed of boards, with its kerosene case paws, as if it had elephantiasis, that bed, and its kidskin, and its dry banana leaves, and its rags, yearning for a mattress, my grandmother's bed (Above the bed, in a jar full of oil a dim light whose flame dances like a fat cockroach . . . on this jar in gold letters: MERCI).*

[27]

And this Straw Street,* this disgrace,
an appendage repulsive as the private parts of the village that extends right and left, along the colonial road, the gray surge of its "shingled" roofs. Here there are only straw roofs, spray-browned and wind-plucked.

[28]

Tout le monde la méprise la rue Paille. C'est là que la jeunesse du bourg se débauche. C'est là surtout que la mer déverse ses immondices, ses chats morts et ses chiens crevés. Car la rue débouche sur la plage, et la plage ne suffit pas à la rage écumante de la mer.

Une détresse cette plage elle aussi, avec ses tas d'ordure pourrissant, ses croupes furtives qui se soulagent, et le sable est noir, funèbre, on n'a jamais vu un sable si noir, et l'écume glisse dessus en glapissant, et la mer la frappe à grands coups de boxe, ou plutôt la mer est un gros chien qui lèche et mord la plage aux jarrets, et à force de la mordre elle finira par la dévorer, bien sûr, la plage et la rue Paille avec.

[29]

Au bout du petit matin, le vent de jadis qui s'élève, des fidélités trahies, du devoir incertain qui se dérobe et cet autre petit matin d'Europe...

[30]

Partir. Mon cœur bruissait de générosités emphatiques. Partir... j'arriverais lisse et jeune dans ce pays mien et je dirais à ce pays dont le limon entre dans la composition de ma chair : « J'ai longtemps erré et je reviens vers la hideur désertée de vos plaies ».

Je viendrais à ce pays mien et je lui dirais : « Embrassez-moi sans crainte... Et si je ne sais que parler, c'est pour vous que je parlerai ».

Et je lui dirais encore :

« Ma bouche sera la bouche des malheurs qui n'ont point de bouche, ma voix, la liberté de celles qui s'affaissent au cachot du désespoir ».

Et venant je me dirais à moi-même :

« Et surtout mon corps aussi bien que mon âme gardez-vous de vous croiser les bras en l'attitude stérile du spectateur, car la vie n'est pas un spectacle, car une mer de douleurs n'est pas un proscenium, car un homme qui crie n'est pas un ours qui danse... ».

Et voici que je suis venu !

[31]

De nouveau cette vie clopinante devant moi, non pas cette vie, cette mort, cette mort sans sens ni piété, cette mort où la grandeur piteusement échoue, l'éclatante petitesse de cette mort, cette mort qui clopine de petitesses en petitesses ; ces pelletées de petites avidités sur le conquistador ;

16

Everyone despises Straw Street. That's where the village youth go bad. It's there especially that the sea pours forth its garbage, its dead cats and croaked dogs. For the street opens onto the beach, and the beach alone cannot satisfy the sea's foaming rage.

A blight this beach as well, with its piles of rotting muck, its furtive rumps relieving themselves, and the sand is black, funereal, you've never seen a sand so black,* and the scum glides over it yelping, and the sea pummels it like a boxer, or rather the sea is a huge dog licking and biting the shins of the beach, biting them so persistently that it will end up devouring it, for sure, the beach and Straw Street along with it.

At the end of first light, the wind of long ago—of betrayed trusts, of uncertain evasive duty and that other dawn in Europe—arises . . .

To leave. My heart was humming with emphatic generosities. To leave. . . . I would arrive sleek and young in this land of mine and I would say to this land whose loam is part of my flesh: "I have wandered for a long time and I am coming back to the deserted hideousness of your sores."

I would come to this land of mine and I would say to it: "Embrace me without fear . . . And if all I can do is speak, it is for you I shall speak."

And again I would say:

"My mouth shall be the mouth of those calamities that have no mouth, my voice the freedom of those who break down in the prison holes of despair."

And on the way I would say to myself:

"And above all, my body as well as my soul beware of assuming the sterile attitude of a spectator, for life is not a spectacle, a sea of miseries is not a proscenium, a man screaming is not a dancing bear . . ."

And behold here I am come home!

Once again this life hobbling before me, what am I saying this life, *this death*, this death without meaning or piety, this death that so pathetically falls short of greatness, the dazzling pettiness of this death, this death hobbling from pettiness to pettiness; these shovelfuls of petty greeds over

ces pelletées de petits larbins sur le grand sauvage, ces pelletées de petites
âmes sur le Caraïbe aux trois âmes,
et toutes ces morts futiles
absurdités sous l'éclaboussement de ma conscience ouverte
tragiques futilités éclairées de cette seule noctiluque
et moi seul, brusque scène de ce petit matin
où fait le beau l'apocalypse des monstres
puis, chavirée, se tait
chaude élection de cendres, de ruines et d'affaissements

[32]

—Encore une objection ! une seule, mais de grâce une seule : je n'ai
pas le droit de calculer la vie à mon empan fuligineux ; de me réduire à
ce petit rien ellipsoïdal qui tremble à quatre doigts au dessus de la ligne,
moi homme d'ainsi bouleverser la création, que je me comprenne entre
latitude et longitude !

[33]

Au bout du petit matin,
la mâle soif et l'entêté désir,
me voici divisé des oasis fraîches de la fraternité
ce rien pudique frise d'échardes dures
cet horizon trop sûr tressaille comme un geôlier.

[34]

Ton dernier triomphe, corbeau tenace de la Trahison.

Ce qui est à moi, ces quelques milliers de mortiférés qui tournent en
rond dans la calebasse d'une île et ce qui est à moi aussi l'archipel arqué
comme le désir inquiet de se nier, on dirait une anxiété maternelle pour
protéger la ténuité plus délicate qui sépare l'une de l'autre Amérique ; et
ses flancs qui sécrètent pour l'Europe la bonne liqueur d'un Gulf Stream,
et l'un des deux versants d'incandescence entre quoi l'Équateur funam-
bule vers l'Afrique. Et mon île non-clôture, sa claire audace debout à
l'arrière de cette polynésie, devant elle, la Guadeloupe fendue en deux de
sa raie dorsale et de même misère que nous, Haïti où la négritude se mit
debout pour la première fois et dit qu'elle croyait à son humanité et la
comique petite queue de la Floride où d'un nègre s'achève la strangula-
tion, et l'Afrique gigantesquement chenillant jusqu'au pied hispanique de
l'Europe, sa nudité où la Mort fauche à larges andains.

the conquistador; these shovelfuls of petty flunkies over the great savage;
these shovelfuls of petty souls over the three-souled Carib,*
and all these deaths futile
absurdities under the splashing of my open conscience
tragic futilities lit up by this single noctiluca
and I alone, sudden stage of this first light
where the apocalypse of monsters cavorts
then, capsized, hushes
warm election of cinders, of ruins and collapses

[32]

—One more thing! only one, but please make it only one; I have no
right to measure life by my sooty finger span; to reduce myself to this little
ellipsoidal nothing trembling four fingers above the line,* I a man to so
overturn creation, that I include myself between latitude and longitude!

[33]

At the end of first light,
the male thirst and the desire stubborn,
here I am, severed from the cool oases of brotherhood
this so modest nothing bristles with hard splinters
this too sure horizon shudders like a jailer.

[34]

Your last triumph, tenacious crow of Treason.

What is mine, these few thousand deathbearers who mill in the cala-
bash of an island and mine too the archipelago arched with an anguished
desire to negate itself, as if from maternal anxiety to protect this impos-
sibly delicate tenuity separating one America from the other; and these
loins which secrete for Europe the hearty liquor of a Gulf Stream, and
one of the two slopes of incandescence between which the Equator tight-
ropewalks toward Africa. And my non-closure island, its brave audacity
standing at the stern of this Polynesia, before it, Guadeloupe split in two
down its dorsal line and equal in poverty to us, Haiti where negritude
rose for the first time* and stated that it believed in its humanity and the
funny little tail of Florida where the strangulation of a nigger is being
completed, and Africa gigantically caterpillaring up to the Hispanic foot
of Europe, its nakedness where Death scythes widely.*

Et je me dis Bordeaux et Nantes et Liverpool
et New-York et San-Francisco
pas un bout de ce monde qui ne porte mon empreinte digitale et mon
calcanéum sur le dos des gratte-ciel et ma crasse dans le scintillement des
gemmes !
Qui peut se vanter d'avoir mieux que moi ?
Virginie. Tennessee. Géorgie. Alabama.
Putréfactions monstrueuses de révoltes inopérantes,
marais de sang putrides
trompettes absurdement bouchées
Terres rouges terres sanguines terres consanguines

Ce qui est à moi aussi : une petite cellule dans le Jura, une petite
cellule, la neige la double de barreaux blancs
la neige est un geôlier blanc qui monte la garde devant une prison
Ce qui est à moi
c'est un homme seul emprisonné de blanc
c'est un homme seul qui défie les cris blancs de la mort blanche
(TOUSSAINT, TOUSSAINT LOUVERTURE)
c'est un homme seul qui fascine l'épervier blanc de la mort blanche
c'est un homme seul dans la mer inféconde de sable blanc
c'est un moricaud vieux dressé contre les eaux du ciel
La mort décrit un cercle brillant au dessus de cet homme
la mort étoile doucement au dessus de sa tête
la mort souffle dans la canne mûre de ses bras
la mort galope dans la prison comme un cheval blanc
la mort luit dans l'ombre comme des yeux de chat
la mort hoquète comme l'eau sous les Cayes
la mort est un oiseau blessé
la mort décroît
la mort vacille
la mort est un patyura ombrageux
la mort expire dans une blanche mare de silence.

  And I say to myself Bordeaux and Nantes and Liverpool
and New York and San Francisco*
not an inch of this world devoid of my fingerprint and my calcaneus on
the spines of skyscrapers and my filth in the glitter of gems!
Who can boast of being better off than I?
Virginia. Tennessee. Georgia. Alabama.
Monstrous putrefactions of revolts stymied,
marshes of putrid blood
trumpets absurdly muted
Land red, sanguineous, consanguineous land

  What is also mine: a little cell in the Jura,* a little cell, the snow lines
it with white bars
the snow is a white jailer mounting guard before a prison
What is mine
a lone man imprisoned in whiteness
a lone man defying the white screams of white death
(TOUSSAINT, TOUSSAINT LOUVERTURE)
a man who mesmerizes the white sparrow hawk of white death
a man alone in the sterile sea of white sand
an old black man standing up to the waters of the sky
Death traces a shining circle above this man
death stars softly above his head
death breathes in the ripened cane of his arms
death gallops in the prison like a white horse
death gleams in the dark like the eyes of a cat
death hiccups like water under the Keys*
death is a struck bird
death wanes
death vacillates
death is a shy patyura*
death expires in a white pool of silence.

[37]

    Gonflements de nuit aux quatre coins de ce petit matin
soubresauts de mort figée
destin tenace
cris debout de terre muette
la splendeur de ce sang n'éclatera-t-elle point ?

[38]

    Et maintenant un dernier zut :
au soleil (Il ne suffit pas à saouler ma tête trop forte)
à la nuit farineuse avec les pondaisons d'or des lucioles incertaines
à la chevelure qui tremble tout au haut de la falaise,
le vent y saute en inconstantes cavaleries salées
je lis bien à mon pouls que l'exotisme n'est pas provende pour moi.

[39]

    Au sortir de l'Europe toute révulsée de cris
les courants silencieux de la désespérance
au sortir de l'Europe peureuse qui se reprend et fière se surestime
je veux cet égoïsme beau et qui s'aventure
et mon labour me remémore d'une implacable étrave.

[40]

Que de sang dans ma mémoire ! Dans ma mémoire sont des lagunes.
Elles sont couvertes de têtes de morts. Elles ne sont pas couvertes de
nénuphars.
Dans ma mémoire sont des lagunes. Sur leurs rives ne sont pas étendus
des pagnes de femmes.
Ma mémoire est entourée de sang. Ma mémoire a sa ceinture de cadavres !

[41]

et mitraille de barils de rhum génialement arrosant
nos révoltes ignobles, pâmoison d'yeux doux
d'avoir lampé la liberté féroce

[42]

(les nègres-sont-tous-les-mêmes, je-vous-le-dis
les vices-tous-les-vices, c'est-moi-qui-vous-le-dis

Swellings of night in the four corners of this first light
convulsions of congealed death
tenacious fate
screams erect from mute earth
the splendor of this blood will it not blast forth?

And now a last raspberry:
to the sun (Not strong enough to inebriate my very tough head)
to the mealy night with its golden hatchings of erratic fireflies
to the chevelure trembling at the very top of the cliff,
where the wind leaps in bursts of salty cavalries
clearly I read in my pulse that for me exoticism is no provender.

Leaving Europe utterly twisted with screams
silent currents of despair
leaving timid Europe which collects and proudly overrates itself
I summon this beautiful egotism that ventures forth
and my ploughing reminds me of an implacable cutwater.

So much blood in my memory! In my memory are lagoons. They are
covered with death's-heads. They are not covered with water lilies.
In my memory are lagoons. No women's loin-cloths spread out on their
shores.
My memory is encircled with blood. My memory has a belt of corpses!

and machine gun fire of rum barrels brilliantly sprinkling
our ignominious revolts, amorous glances swooning
from having swigged too much ferocious freedom

(niggers-are-all-alike, I-tell-you
vices-all-the-vices, believe-you-me

l'odeur-du-nègre, ça-fait-pousser-la-canne
rappelez-vous-le-vieux-dicton :
battre-un-nègre, c'est le nourrir)

[43]

autour des rocking-chairs méditant la volupté des rigoises. . .

[44]

Je tourne, inapaisée pouliche
Ou bien tout simplement comme on nous aime !
Obscènes gaiement, très doudous de jazz sur leur excès d'ennui.
Je sais le tracking, le Lindy-hop et les claquettes.
Pour les bonnes bouches la sourdine de nos plaintes enrobées de oua-
oua. Attendez. . .
Tout est dans l'ordre. Mon bon ange broute du néon. J'avale des
baguettes. Ma dignité
se vautre dans les dégobillements. . .

[45]

   Soleil, Ange Soleil, Ange frisé du Soleil.
   Pour un bond par delà la nage verdâtre et douce des eaux de l'abjection !
   Mais je me suis adressé au mauvais sorcier. Sur cette terre exorcisée,
larguée à la dérive de sa précieuse intention maléfique, cette voix qui
crie, lentement enrouée, vainement, vainement enrouée, et il n'y a que les
fientes accumulées de nos mensonges—et qui ne répondent pas.

[46]

Quelle folie le merveilleux entrechat par moi rêvé au dessus de la
bassesse !
Parbleu les Blancs sont de grands guerriers
hosannah pour le maître et pour le châtre-nègre !
Victoire ! Victoire vous dis-je : les vaincus sont contents !
Joyeuses puanteurs et chants de boue !

[47]

   Par une inattendue et bienfaisante révolution intérieure j'honore main-
tenant mes laideurs repoussantes.

nigger-smell, that's-what-makes-cane-grow
remember-the-old-saying:
beat-a-nigger, and you feed him)

[43]

around rocking chairs contemplating the voluptousness of quirts . . .

[44]

I circle about, an unappeased filly
Or quite simply as they love to see us!
Cheerfully obscene, completely nuts about jazz to cover their extreme
boredom.
I can boogie-woogie, do the Lindy-hop and tap dance.
For a special treat our groans muffled with wah-wah. Wait...
Everything is as it should be. My good angel grazes the neon. I swallow
drumsticks. My dignity wallows in puke . . .

[45]

Sun, Angel Sun, curly Angel of the Sun.

For a leap beyond the sweet and greenish sculling of the waters of
abjection!

But I approached the wrong sorcerer. On this exorcised earth, cast
adrift from its precious malignant purpose, this voice that cries, little by
little hoarse, vainly, vainly hoarse, and there remain only the accumulated
droppings of our lies—and they do not respond.

[46]

What madness to dream up a marvelous entrechat above the baseness!
By Gad the Whites are great warriors
hosannah to the master and to the nigger-gelder!
Victory! Victory I tell you: the conquered are content!
Joyous stenches and songs of mud!

[47]

By a sudden and beneficent inner revolution I now honor my repugnant
ugliness.

À la Saint-Jean-Baptiste, dès que tombent les premières ombres sur le bourg du Gros-Morne, des centaines de maquignons se réunissent pour échanger leurs chevaux, dans la rue « DE PROFUNDIS » dont le nom a du moins la franchise d'avertir d'une ruée des bas-fonds de la Mort. Et c'est de la Mort véritablement, de ses mille mesquines formes locales (fringales inassouvies d'herbe de Para et rond asservissement des distilleries) que surgit vers la grand'vie déclose l'étonnante cavalerie des rosses impétueuses. Et quels galops ! quels hennissements ! quelles sincères urines ! quelles fientes mirobolantes ! « Un beau cheval difficile au montoiṛ ! » — « Une altière jument sensible à la molette ! » — « Un intrépide poulain vaillamment jointé ! »

Et le malin compère dont le gilet se barre d'une fière chaîne de montre, refile au lieu de pleines mamelles, d'ardeurs juvéniles, de rotondités authentiques, ou les boursouflures régulières de guêpes complaisantes, ou les obscènes morsures du gingembre, ou la bienfaisante circulation d'un décalitre d'eau sucrée.

Je refuse de me donner mes boursouflures comme d'authentiques gloires.

Et je ris de mes anciennes imaginations puériles.

Non, nous n'avons jamais été amazones du roi de Dahomey, ni princes de Ghana avec huit cents chameaux, ni docteurs à Tombouctou Askia le Grand étant roi, ni architectes de Djéné, ni Madhis, ni guerriers. Nous ne nous sentons pas sous l'aisselle la démangeaison de ceux qui tinrent jadis la lance. Et puisque j'ai juré de ne rien celer de notre histoire, (moi qui n'admire rien tant que le mouton broutant son ombre d'après-midi), je veux avouer que nous fûmes de tout temps d'assez piètres laveurs de vaisselle, des cireurs de chaussures sans envergure, mettons les choses au mieux, d'assez consciencieux sorciers et le seul indiscutable record que nous ayons battu est celui d'endurance à la chicotte...

Et ce pays cria pendant des siècles que nous sommes des bêtes brutes ; que les pulsations de l'humanité s'arrêtent aux portes de la négrerie ; que nous sommes un fumier ambulant hideusement prometteur de cannes tendres et de coton soyeux et l'on nous marquait au fer rouge et nous dormions dans nos excréments et l'on nous vendait sur les places et l'aune de drap anglais et la viande salée d'Irlande coûtaient moins cher

On Midsummer Day, as soon as the first shadows fall across the village of Gros-Morne, hundreds of dealers gather to exchange their horses on rue "DE PROFUNDIS" a name at least honest enough to announce an onrush from the shoals of Death. And truly it is from Death, from its thousand petty local forms (cravings unsatisfied by Para grass and tipsy bondage to the distilleries) that the astonishing cavalry of impetuous nags surges unenclosed toward the great-life. What galloping! what neighing! What sincere urinating! What prodigious droppings! "A fine horse difficult to mount!"—"A proud mare sensitive to the spur!"—"A fearless foal superbly pasterned!"

And the shrewd fellow whose waistcoat displays a proud watch chain, palms off, instead of full udders, youthful mettle, genuine contours, either the systematic puffiness from obliging wasps, or obscene stings from ginger, or the helpful distribution of several gallons of sugared water.

I refuse to pass off my puffiness for authentic glory.

And I laugh at my former puerile fantasies.

No, we've never been Amazons of the king of Dahomey,* nor princes of Ghana with eight hundred camels, nor wise men in Timbuktu under Askia the Great,* nor the architects of Djenne,* nor Madhis,* nor warriors. We don't feel under our armpit the itch of those who in the old days carried a lance. And since I have sworn to leave nothing out of our history (I who love nothing better than a sheep grazing his own afternoon shadow), I may as well confess that we were at all times pretty mediocre dishwashers, shoeblacks without ambition, at best conscientious sorcerers and the only unquestionable record that we broke was that of endurance under the chicote . . .*

And this land screamed for centuries that we are bestial brutes; that the human pulse stops at the gates of the barracoon; that we are walking compost hideously promising tender cane and silky cotton and they would brand us with red-hot irons and we would sleep in our excrement and they would sell us on the town square and an ell of English cloth and

que nous, et ce pays était calme, tranquille, disant que l'esprit de Dieu était dans ses actes.

[50]

Le négrier ! proclame mon sûr et ténébreux instinct, les voiles de noires nuages, la polymâture de forêts sombres et des dures magnificences des Calebars, insigne souvenir à la proue blanchoyant—ce squelette !

[51]

J'entends de la cale monter les malédictions enchaînées, les hoquètements des mourants, le bruit d'un qu'on jette à la mer. . . les abois d'une femme en gésine. . . des râclements d'ongles cherchant des gorges. . . des ricanements de fouet. . . des farfouillis de vermines parmi des lassitudes. . .

[52]

Rien ne put nous insurger jamais vers quelque noble aventure désespérée.
Ainsi soit-il. Ainsi soit-il.
Je ne suis d'aucune nationalité prévue par les chancelleries
Je défie le craniomètre. Homo sum etc. . . .
Et qu'ils servent et trahissent et meurent
Ainsi soit-il. Ainsi soit-il. C'était écrit dans la forme de leur bassin.
Et moi, et moi,
moi qui chantai le poing dur
Il faut savoir jusqu'où je poussai la lâcheté.
Un soir dans un tramway en face de moi, un nègre.
C'était un nègre grand comme un pongo qui essayait de se faire tout petit sur un banc de tramway. Il essayait d'abandonner sur ce banc crasseux de tramway ses jambes gigantesques et ses mains tremblantes de boxeur affamé. Et tout l'avait laissé, le laissait. Son nez qui semblait une péninsule en dérade et sa négritude même qui se décolorait sous l'action d'une inlassable mégie. Et le mégissier était la Misère. Un gros oreillard subit dont les coups de griffes sur ce visage s'étaient cicatrisés en îlots scabieux. Ou plutôt c'était un ouvrier infatigable, la Misère, travaillant à quelque cartouche hideux. On voyait très bien comment le pouce industrieux et malveillant avait modelé le front en bosse, percé le nez de deux tunnels parallèles et inquiétants, allongé la démesure de la lippe, et par un chef-d'œuvre caricatural, raboté, poli, verni la plus minuscule mignonne petite oreille de la création.

salted meat from Ireland cost less than we did, and this land was calm, tranquil, repeating that the spirit of the Lord was in its acts.

[50]

The slave ship! proclaim my certain and darkest instincts, the sails of black clouds, the polymasting of somber forests and the Calebars' harsh magnificence, a glaring memory of the whitening prow—this skeleton!

[51]

I hear coming up from the hold enchained curses, the death gasps of the dying, the sound of someone thrown into the sea . . . the baying of a woman in labor . . . the scraping of fingernails searching for throats . . . the flouts of the whip . . . the seething of vermin amidst the weariness . . .

[52]

Nothing could ever lift us toward a noble hopeless adventure.
So be it. So be it.
I am of no nationality recognized by the chancelleries
I defy the craniometer. Homo sum etc. . . .
Let them serve and betray and die
So be it. So be it. It was written in the shape of their pelvis.*
And I, and I,
I was singing the hard fist
You must know the extent of my cowardice.
One evening on the streetcar facing me, a nigger.
    A nigger big as a pongo trying to make himself small on the streetcar bench. He was trying to leave behind on this grimy bench his gigantic legs and his trembling famished boxer hands. And everything had left him, was leaving him. His nose which looked like a drifting peninsula and even his negritude discolored as a result of untiring tawing. And the tawer was Poverty. A big unexpected lop-eared bat whose claw marks in his face had scabbed over into crusty islands. Or rather, Poverty was, like a tireless worker, laboring over some hideous cartouche. One could easily see how that industrious and malevolent thumb had kneaded bumps into his brow, bored two parallel and troubling tunnels in his nose, over-exaggerated his lips, and in a masterpiece of caricature, planed, polished, and varnished the tiniest cutest little ear in all creation.

C'était un nègre dégingandé sans rythme ni mesure.

Un nègre à la voix embrumée d'alcool et de misère.

Un nègre dont les yeux roulaient une lassitude sanguinolante.

Un nègre sans pudeur et ses orteils ricanaient de façon assez puante au fond de la tanière entrebâillée de ses souliers.

La Misère, on ne pouvait pas dire, s'était donné un mal fou pour l'achever.

Elle avait creusé l'orbite, l'avait fardée d'un fard de poussière et de chassie mêlées.

Elle avait tendu l'espace vide entre l'accrochement solide des mâchoires et les pommettes d'une vieille joue décatie. Elle avait planté dessus les petits pieux luisants d'une barbe de plusieurs jours. Elle avait affolé le cœur, voûté le dos.

Et l'ensemble faisait parfaitement un nègre hideux, un nègre grognon, un nègre mélancolique, un nègre affalé, ses mains réunies en prière sur un bâton noueux. Un nègre enseveli dans une vieille veste élimée. Un nègre comique et laid et des femmes derrière moi ricanaient en le regardant.

Moi je me tournai, mes yeux proclamant que je n'avais rien de commun avec ce singe.

Il était COMIQUE ET LAID,

COMIQUE ET LAID pour sûr.

J'arborai un grand sourire complice. . .

Ma lâcheté retrouvée !

Je salue les trois siècles qui soutiennent mes droits civiques et mon sang minimisé.

Mon héroïsme, quelle farce !

Cette ville est à ma taille.

Et mon âme est couchée. Comme cette ville dans la crasse et dans la boue couchée.

Cette ville, ma face de boue.

L'eau du baptême sur mon front se sèche.

Je réclame pour ma face la louange éclatante du crachat ! . . .

Alors, nous étant tels, à nous l'élan viril, le genou vainqueur, les plaines à grosses mottes de l'avenir !

Tiens, je préfère avouer que j'ai généreusement déliré, mon cœur dans ma cervelle ainsi qu'un genou ivre.

He was a gangly nigger without rhythm or measure.

A nigger with a voice fogged over by alcohol and poverty.

A nigger whose eyes rolled a bloodshot weariness.

A shameless nigger and his toes sneered in a rather stinking way at the bottom of the yawning lair of his shoes.

Poverty, without any question, had knocked itself out to finish him off.

It had dug the socket, had painted it with a rouge of dust mixed with rheum.

It had stretched an empty space between the solid hinge of the jaw and the bones in an old tarnished cheek. Had planted over it the small shiny stakes of a two- or three-day beard. Had panicked his heart, bent his back.

And the whole thing added up perfectly to a hideous nigger, a grouchy nigger, a melancholy nigger, a slouched nigger, his hands joined in prayer on a knobby stick. A nigger shrouded in an old threadbare coat. A comical and ugly nigger, with some women behind me sneering at him.

Me I turned, my eyes proclaiming that I had nothing in common with this monkey.

He was COMICAL AND UGLY,*

COMICAL AND UGLY for sure.

I displayed a big complicitous smile . . .

My cowardice rediscovered!

Hail to the three centuries that uphold my civil rights and my minimized blood.

My heroism, what a farce!

This town fits me to a t.

And my soul is prostrate. Prostrate like this town in its refuse and mud.

This town, my face of mud.

The baptismal water dries on my forehead.

For my face I demand the vivid homage of spit! . . .

So, being what we are, ours the warrior thrust, the triumphant knee, the well-plowed plains of the future!

Look, I'd rather admit to uninhibited ravings, my heart in my brain like a drunken knee.

Mon étoile maintenant, le menfenil funèbre.

Et sur ce rêve ancien mes cruautés cannibales.
Les balles sont dans la bouche salive épaisse
notre cœur de quotidienne bassesse éclate
les continents rompent la frêle attache des isthmes
des terres sautent suivant la division fatale des fleuves
et le morne qui depuis des siècles retient son cri au dedans de lui-même,
c'est lui qui à son tour écartèle le
silence
et ce peuple vaillance rebondissante !
et nos membres vainement disjoints par les plus raffinés supplices, et
la vie plus impétueuse jaillissant de ce fumier—comme le corrossolier
imprévu de la décomposition des fruits du jacquier !

Sur ce rêve vieux en moi mes cruautés cannibales

Je me cachais derrière une vanité stupide
le destin m'appelait j'étais caché derrière
et voici l'homme par terre ! Sa très fragile défense dispersée,
ses maximes sacrées foulées aux pieds, ses déclamations pédantesques
rendant du vent par chaque blessure.
Voici l'homme par terre
et son âme est comme nue
et le destin triomphe qui contemple se muer
en l'ancestral bourbier cette âme qui le défiait.

Je dis que cela est bien ainsi.
Mon dos exploitera victorieusement la chalasie des fibres.
Je pavoiserai de reconnaissance mon obséquiosité naturelle
Et rendra des points à mon enthousiasme le boniment galonné d'argent
du postillon de la Havane, lyrique babouin entremetteur des splendeurs
de la servitude.

[53]

My star now, the funereal menfenil.*

[54]

And on this former dream my cannibalistic cruelties.
Bullets are in the mouth thick saliva
our heart from daily lowness bursts
the continents break the fragile bond of isthmuses
lands explode in accordance with the fatal division of rivers
and the morne which for centuries kept its scream within itself, draws
and quarters the
silence in its turn
and this people an ever-rebounding valor!
and our limbs vainly disjointed by the most refined tortures, and life
even more impetuously springing up from this dunghill—unexpected as
a soursop amidst the decomposition of breadfruit!

[55]

On this dream so old in me my cannibalistic cruelties

[56]

I was hiding behind a stupid vanity
destiny called me I was hiding behind it
and suddenly there was man on the ground! His feeble defenses
scattered,
his sacred maxims trampled underfoot, his pedantic rhetoric so much
hot air through each wound.
There was man on the ground
and his soul appears naked
and destiny triumphs in watching this soul which
defied its metamorphosis in the ancestral quagmire.

[57]

I say that this is right.
My back will victoriously exploit the chalaza of fibers.
I will deck out my natural obsequiousness with gratitude
And the silver-braided bullshit of the postillion* of Havana, lyric
baboon pimp for the glamour of slavery, will be more than a match for
my enthusiasm.

[58]

Je dis que cela est bien ainsi.
Je vis pour le plus plat de mon âme.
Pour le plus terne de ma chair !

[59]

   Tiède petit matin de chaleur et de peur ancestrales
je tremble maintenant du commun tremblement
que notre sang docile chante dans le madrépore.

[60]

Et ces têtards en moi éclos de mon ascendance prodigieuse !

[61]

ceux qui n'ont inventé ni la poudre ni la boussole
ceux qui n'ont jamais su dompter la vapeur ni l'électricité
ceux qui n'ont exploré ni les mers ni le ciel
mais ils savent en ses moindres recoins le pays de souffrance
ceux qui n'ont connu de voyages que de déracinements
ceux qui se sont assouplis aux agenouillements
ceux qu'on domestiqua et christianisa
ceux qu'on inocula d'abâtardissement
tam-tams de mains vides
tam-tams inanes de plaies sonores
tam-tams burlesques de trahison tabide

[62]

   Tiède petit matin de chaleurs et de peurs ancestrales
par dessus bord mes richesses pérégrines
par dessus bord mes faussetés authentiques

[63]

Mais quel étrange orgueil tout soudain m'illumine?

[64]

O lumière amicale
O fraîche source de lumière
ceux qui n'ont inventé ni la poudre ni la boussole

34

[58]

I say that this is right.
I live for the flattest part of my soul.
For the dullest part of my flesh!

[59]

Tepid first light of ancestral heat and fear
I now tremble with the collective trembling
that our blood sings in the madrepore.

[60]

And these tadpoles hatched in me by my prodigious ancestry!

[61]

those who invented neither powder nor compass
those who could harness neither steam nor electricity
those who explored neither the seas nor the sky
but knew in its most minute corners the land of suffering
those who have known voyages only through uprootings
those who have been lulled to sleep by so much kneeling
those whom they domesticated and Christianized
those whom they inoculated with degeneracy
tom-toms of empty hands
inane tom-toms of resounding sores
burlesque tom-toms of tabetic treason

[62]

Tepid first light of ancestral heat and fear
overboard with my alien riches
overboard with my genuine falseness

[63]

But what strange pride of a sudden illuminates me?

[64]

O friendly light
O fresh source of light
those who invented neither powder nor compass

ceux qui n'ont jamais su dompter la vapeur ni l'électricité
ceux qui n'ont exploré ni les mers ni le ciel
maix ceux sans qui la terre ne serait pas la terre
gibbosité d'autant plus bienfaisante que la terre déserte davantage la
terre
silo où se préserve et mûrit ce que la terre a de plus terre
ma négritude n'est pas une pierre, sa surdité ruée contre la clameur du
jour
ma négritude n'est pas une taie d'eau morte sur l'œil mort de la terre
ma négritude n'est ni une tour ni une cathédrale

[65]

elle plonge dans la chair rouge du sol
elle plonge dans la chair ardente du ciel
elle troue l'accablement opaque de sa droite patience.

[66]

Eia pour le Kaïlcédrat royal !
Eia pour ceux qui n'ont jamais rien inventé
pour ceux qui n'ont jamais rien exploré
pour ceux qui n'ont jamais rien dompté

[67]

mais ils s'abandonnent, saisis, à l'essence de toutes choses
ignorants des surfaces mais saisis par le mouvement de toutes choses
insoucieux de dompter, mais jouant le jeu du monde
véritablement les fils aînés du monde
poreux à tous les souffles du monde
aire fraternelle de tous les souffles du monde
lit sans drain de toutes les eaux du monde
étincelle du feu sacré du monde
chair de la chair du monde palpitant du mouvement même du monde !

[68]

Tiède petit matin de vertus ancestrales
Sang ! Sang ! tout notre sang ému par le cœur mâle du soleil
ceux qui savent la féminité de la lune au corps d'huile

those who could harness neither steam nor electricity
those who explored neither the seas nor the sky
but those without whom the earth would not be the earth
gibbosity all the more beneficent as more and more the earth deserts the
earth
silo where that which is earthiest about earth ferments and ripens
my negritude is not a stone, its deafness hurled against the clamor of the
day
my negritude is not a leukoma of dead liquid over the earth's dead eye
my negritude is neither tower nor cathedral

[65]

it takes root in the red flesh of the soil
it takes root in the ardent flesh of the sky
it breaks through opaque prostration with its upright patience.

[66]

Eia for the royal Cailcedra!*
Eia for those who never invented anything
for those who never explored anything
for those who never conquered anything

[67]

but who yield, seized, to the essence of all things*
ignorant of surfaces but captivated by the motion of all things
indifferent to conquering, but playing the game of the world
truly the eldest sons of the world
porous to all the breathing of the world
fraternal locus for all the breathing of the world
drainless channel for all the water of the world
spark of the sacred fire of the world
flesh of the world's flesh pulsating with the very motion of the world!

[68]

   Tepid first light of ancestral virtues
Blood! Blood! all our blood aroused by the male heart of the sun
those who know about the femininity of the moon's oily body

l'exaltation réconciliée de l'antilope et de l'étoile
ceux dont la survie chemine en la germination de l'herbe !

[69]

Eia parfait cercle du monde et close concordance !

[70]

Écoutez le monde blanc
horriblement las de son effort immense
ses articulations rebelles craquer sous les étoiles dures
ses raideurs d'acier bleu transperçant la chair mystique
écoute ses victoires proditoires trompetter ses défaites
écoute aux alibis grandioses son piètre trébuchement

[71]

Pitié pour nos vainqueurs omniscients et naïfs !

[72]

Eia pour ceux qui n'ont jamais rien inventé
pour ceux qui n'ont jamais rien exploré
pour ceux qui n'ont jamais rien dompté

[73]

Eia pour la joie
Eia pour l'amour
Eia pour la douleur aux pis de larmes réincarnées

[74]

Et voici au bout de ce petit matin ma prière virile
que je n'entende ni les rires ni les cris, les yeux fixés sur cette ville que je
prophétise, belle,

[75]

donnez-moi le courage du martyr
donnez-moi la foi sauvage du sorcier
donnez à mes mains puissance de modeler
donnez à mon âme la trempe de l'épée
je ne me dérobe point. Faites de ma tête une tête de proue

the reconciled exultation of antelope and star
those whose survival walks on the germination of the grass!

[69]

Eia perfect circle of the world and enclosed concordance!

[70]

Hear the white world
horribly weary from its immense effort
its rebellious joints cracking under the hard stars
its blue steel rigidities piercing the mystic flesh
hear its proditorious victories touting its defeats
hear the grandiose alibis for its pitiful stumbling

[71]

Pity for our omniscient and naïve conquerors!

[72]

Eia for those who never invented anything
for those who never explored anything
for those who never conquered anything

[73]
Eia for joy
Eia for love
Eia for grief and its dugs of reincarnated tears

[74]

And here at the end of this first light my virile prayer
that I hear neither the laughter nor the screams, my eyes fixed on this
town that I prophesy, beautiful,

[75]

grant me the courage of the martyr
grant me the savage faith of the sorcerer
grant my hands the power to mold
grant my soul the sword's temper
I won't flinch. Make my head into a figurehead

et de moi-même, mon cœur, ne faites ni un père ni un frère,
ni un fils, mais le père mais le frère, mais le fils,
ni un mari, mais l'amant de cet unique peuple.

[76]

Faites-moi rebelle à toute vanité, mais docile à son génie comme le
poing à l'allongée du bras !
Faites-moi commissaire de son sang
faites-moi dépositaire de son ressentiment
faites de moi un homme de terminaison
faites de moi un homme d'initiation
faites de moi un homme de recueillement
mais faites aussi de moi un homme d'ensemencement

[77]

faites de moi l'exécuteur de ces œuvres hautes

[78]

voici le temps de se ceindre les reins comme un vaillant homme.

[79]

Mais les faisant, mon cœur, préservez-moi de toute haine
ne faites point de moi cet homme de haine pour qui je n'ai que haine
car pour me cantonner en cette unique race
vous savez pourtant mon amour catholique
vous savez que ce n'est point par haine des autres races
que je m'exige bêcheur de cette unique race
que ce que je veux
c'est pour la faim universelle
pour la soif universelle

[80]

la sommer libre enfin

[81]

de produire de son intimité close
la succulence des fruits.

and as for me, my heart, make me not into a father nor a brother,
nor a son, but into the father, the brother, the son,
nor a husband, but the lover of this unique people.

Make me resist all vanity, but espouse its genius like the fist the
extended arm!
Make me a steward of its blood
make me a trustee of its resentment
make me into a man of termination
make me into a man of initiation
make me into a man of meditation
but also make me into a man of germination

make me into the executor of these lofty works

the time has come to gird one's loins like a brave man.*

But in doing so, my heart, preserve me from all hatred
do not make me into that man of hatred for whom I feel only hatred
for sheltered as I am in this unique race
you still know my catholic love
you know that it is not from hatred of other races
that I demand of myself to be a digger for this unique race
that what I want
is for universal hunger
for universal thirst

to summon it free at last

to generate from its intimate closeness
the succulence of fruit.

Et voyez l'arbre de nos mains !
il tourne pour tous, les blessures incises en son tronc
pour tous le sol travaille
et griserie vers les branches de précipitation parfumée !

Mais avant d'aborder aux futurs vergers
donnez-moi de les mériter sur leur ceinture de mer
donnez-moi mon cœur en attendant le sol
donnez-moi sur l'océan stérile
mais où caresse la main la promesse de l'amure
donnez-moi sur cet océan divers
l'obstination de la fière pirogue
et sa vigueur marine.

La voici avancer par escalades et retombées sur le flot pulvérisé
la voici danser la danse sacrée devant la grisaille du bourg
la voici barir d'un lambi vertigineux
voici galoper le lambi jusqu'à l'indécision des mornes
et voici par vingt fois d'un labour vigoureux la pagaie forcer l'eau
la pirogue se cabre sous l'assaut de la lame, dévie un instant,
tente de fuir, mais la caresse rude de la pagaie la vire,
alors elle fonce, un frémissement parcourt l'échine de la vague,
la mer bave et gronde
la pirogue comme un traîneau file sur le sable.

Au bout de ce petit matin, ma prière virile :

donnez-moi les muscles de cette pirogue sur la mer démontée et
l'allégresse convaincante du lambi de la bonne nouvelle !

Tenez je ne suis plus qu'un homme (aucune dégradation, aucun crachat
ne le conturbe)

[82]

And see the tree of our hands!
it turns for all, the wounds cut in its trunk*
the soil works for all
and toward the branches a headiness of fragrant precipitation!

[83]

But before reaching the shores of future orchards
grant that I deserve those on their belt of sea
grant me my heart while awaiting the earth
grant me on the ocean sterile
but somewhere caressed by the promise of the clew-line
grant me on this diverse ocean
the obstinacy of the proud pirogue
and its marine vigor.

[84]

See it advance rising and falling on the pulverized wave
see it dance the sacred dance before the grayness of the village
see it trumpet from a vertiginous conch
see the conch gallop up to the uncertainty of the mornes
and see twenty times over the paddles vigorously plow the water
the pirogue rears under the attack of the swells, deviates for an instant,
tries to escape, but the paddle's rough caress turns it,
then it charges, a shudder runs along the wave's spine,
the sea slobbers and rumbles
the pirogue like a sleigh glides onto the sand.

[85]

  At the end of this first light, my virile prayer:

[86]

grant me pirogue muscles on this raging sea and the irresistible gaiety of
the conch of good tidings!

[87]

Look, now I am only a man (no degradation, no spit perturbs him)*
now I am only a man who accepts emptied of anger

je ne suis plus qu'un homme qui accepte n'ayant plus de colère
(il n'a plus dans le cœur que de l'amour immense)
J'accepte. . . J'accepte. . . entièrement, sans réserve. . .
ma race qu'aucune ablution d'hysope et de lys mêlés ne pourrait purifier
ma race rongée de macules
ma race raisin mûr pour pieds ivres
ma reine des crachats et des lèpres
ma reine des fouets et des scrofules
ma reine des squasmes des chloasmes
(oh ces reines que j'aimais jadis aux jardins printaniers et lointains avec
derrière l'illumination de toutes les bougies de marronniers !).
J'accepte. J'accepte.
et le nègre fustigé qui dit : « Pardon mon maître »
et les vingt-neuf coups de fouet légal
et le cachot de quatre pieds de haut
et le carcan à branches
et le jarret coupé à mon audace marronne
et la fleur de lys qui flue du fer rouge sur le gras de mon épaule
et la niche de Monsieur VAULTIER MAYENCOURT, où j'aboyai six mois
de caniche
et Monsieur BRAFIN
et Monsieur de FOURNIOL
et Monsieur de la MAHAUDIÈRE
et le pian
le molosse
le suicide
la promiscuité
le brodequin
le cep
le chevalet
le cippe
le frontal

[88]

Et mon originale géographie aussi ; la carte du monde faite à mon usage,
non pas teinte aux arbitraires couleurs des savants, mais à la géométrie
de mon sang répandu

(nothing left in his heart but immense love)
I accept . . . I accept . . . totally, without reservation . . .*
my race that no ablution of hyssop mixed with lilies could purify*
my race pitted with blemishes
my race ripe grapes for drunken feet*
my queen of spittle and leprosy
my queen of whips and scrofula
my queen of squama and chloasma
(oh those queens I once loved in the remote gardens of spring against
the illumination of all the candles of the chestnut trees!).*
I accept. I accept.
and the flogged nigger saying "Forgive me master"
and the twenty-nine legal blows of the whip*
and the four-foot-high prison cell
and the spiked carcan
and the hamstringing of my runaway audacity
and the fleur de lys flowing from the red iron into the fat of my
shoulder*
and Monsieur VAULTIER MAYENCOURT's kennel where I barked six
poodle months
and Monsieur BRAFIN
and Monsieur FOURNIOL
and Monsieur de la MAHAUDIÈRE
and the yaws
the mastiff
the suicide
the promiscuity
the bootkin
the shackles
the rack
the cippus
the headscrew

[88]

And my special geography too; the world map made for my own use, not
tinted with the arbitrary colors of scholars, but with the geometry of my
spilled blood

45

[89]

et la détermination de ma biologie non prisonnière d'un angle facial, d'une forme de cheveux, d'un nez suffisamment aplati, d'un teint suffisamment mélanien, et la négritude, non plus un indice céphalique, ou un plasma, ou un soma, mais mesurée au compas de la souffrance

[90]

et le nègre chaque jour plus bas, plus lâche, plus stérile, moins profond, plus répandu au dehors, plus séparé de soi-même, plus rusé avec soi-même, moins immédiat avec soi-même

[91]

j'accepte, j'accepte tout cela

[92]

et loin de la mer de palais qui déferle sous la syzygie suppurante des ampoules, merveilleusement couché le corps de mon pays dans le désespoir de mes bras, ses os ébranlés et dans ses veines le sang qui hésite comme la goutte de lait végétal à la pointe blessée du bulbe. . . Et voici soudain que force et vie m'assaillent comme un taureau et je renouvelle ONAN qui confia son sperme à la terre féconde et l'onde de vie circonvient la papille du morne, et voilà toutes les veines et veinules qui s'affairent au sang neuf et l'énorme poumon des cyclones qui respire et le feu thésaurisé des volcans et le gigantesque pouls sismique qui bat maintenant la mesure d'un corps vivant en mon ferme embrassement.

[93]

Et nous sommes debout maintenant, mon pays et moi, les cheveux dans le vent, ma main petite maintenant dans son poing énorme et la force n'est pas en nous, mais au dessus de nous, dans une voix qui vrille la nuit et l'audience comme la pénétrance d'une guêpe apocalyptique.
Et la voix prononce que l'Europe nous a pendant des siècles gavés de mensonges et gonflés de pestilences,
car il n'est point vrai que l'œuvre de l'homme est finie
que nous n'avons rien à faire au monde
que nous parasitons le monde
qu'il suffit que nous nous mettions au pas du monde

[89]

and the determination of my biology* not a prisoner to a facial angle, to a type of hair, to a well-flattened nose, to a clearly melanian coloring, and negritude, no longer a cephalic index, or plasma, or soma, but measured by the compass of suffering

[90]

and the Negro every day more base, more cowardly, more sterile, less profound, more spilled out of himself, more separated from himself, more wily with himself, less immediate to himself

[91]

I accept, I accept it all

[92]

and far from the palatial sea that foams under the suppurating syzygy of blisters, the body of my country miraculously laid in the despair of my arms*, its bones shattered and in its veins, the blood hesitating like a drop of vegetal milk at the injured point of a bulb... Suddenly now strength and life assail me like a bull and I revive ONAN* who entrusted his sperm to the fecund earth and the water of life circumvents the papilla of the morne, and now all the veins and veinlets are bustling with new blood and the enormous breathing lung of cyclones and the fire hoarded in volcanoes and the gigantic seismic pulse that now beats the measure of a living body in my firm embrace.

[93]

And we are standing now, my country and I, hair in the wind, my hand puny in its enormous fist and the strength is not in us, but above us, in a voice that drills the night and the hearing like the penetrance of an apocalyptic wasp.*
And the voice proclaims that for centuries Europe has force-fed us with lies and bloated us with pestilence,
for it is not true that the work of man is done
that we have no business being in the world
that we parasite the world
that it is enough for us to heel to the world

[94]

mais l'œuvre de l'homme vient seulement de commencer

[95]

et il reste à l'homme à conquérir toute interdiction immobilisée aux coins de sa ferveur
et aucune race ne possède le monopole de la beauté, de l'intelligence, de la force
et il est place pour tous au rendez-vous de la conquête et nous savons maintenant que le soleil tourne autour de notre terre éclairant la parcelle qu'a fixée notre volonté seule et que toute étoile chute de ciel en terre à notre commandement sans limite.

[96]

Je tiens maintenant le sens de l'ordalie : mon pays est la « lance de nuit » de mes ancêtres Bambaras.
Elle se ratatine et sa pointe fuit désespérément vers le manche si c'est de sang de poulet qu'on l'arrose et elle dit que c'est du sang d'homme qu'il faut à son tempérament, de la graisse, du foie, du cœur d'homme, non du sang de poulet.
Et je cherche pour mon pays non des cœurs de datte, mais des cœurs d'homme qui c'est pour entrer aux villes d'argent par la grand'porte trapézoïdale qu'ils battent le sang viril, et mes yeux balayent mes kilomètres carrés de terre paternelle et je dénombre les plaies avec une sorte d'allégresse et je les entasse l'une sur l'autre comme rares espèces, et mon compte s'allonge toujours d'imprévus monnayages de la bassesse.
Et voici ceux qui ne se consolent point de n'être pas faits à la ressemblance de Dieu mais du diable, ceux qui considèrent que l'on est nègre comme commis de seconde classe : en attendant mieux et avec possibilité de monter plus haut ; ceux qui battent la chamade devant soi-même, ceux qui vivent dans un cul de basse fosse de soi-même ; ceux qui se drapent de pseudomorphose fière ; ceux qui disent à l'Europe : « Voyez, je sais comme vous faire des courbettes, comme vous présenter mes hommages, en somme je ne suis pas différent de vous ; ne faites pas attention à ma peau noire : c'est le soleil qui m'a brûlé ».
Et il y a le maquereau nègre, l'askari nègre, et tous zèbres se secouent à leur manière pour faire tomber leurs zébrures en une rosée de lait frais.

whereas the work of man has only begun

and man still must overcome all the interdictions wedged in the recesses
of his fervor
and no race has a monopoly on beauty, on intelligence, on strength
and there is room for everyone at the convocation of conquest and we
know now that the sun turns around our earth lighting the parcel desig-
nated by our will alone and that every star falls from sky to earth at our
omnipotent command.

I now see the meaning of this ordeal: my country is the "lance of night"
of my Bambara ancestors.*
It shrinks and its tip desperately retreats toward the haft when it is
sprinkled with chicken blood and it states that its temperament requires
the blood of man, his fat, his liver, his heart, not chicken blood.
And I seek for my country not date hearts, but men's hearts which in
order to enter the silver cities through the great trapezoidal gate beat
with virile blood, and as my eyes sweep my kilometers of paternal earth
I number its sores almost joyfully and I pile one on top of another like
rare species, and my total is ever lengthened by unexpected mintings of
baseness.
And there are those who will never get over not being made in the like-
ness of God but of the devil, those who believe that being a nigger is
like being a second-class clerk: waiting for a better deal and upward
mobility; those who bang the chamade before themselves, those who live
in a corner of their own deep pit; those who drape themselves in proud
pseudomorphosis;* those who say to Europe: "You see I *can* bow and
scrape, like you I pay my respects, in short I am not different from you;
pay no attention to my black skin: the sun did it.*"
And there is the nigger pimp, the nigger askari, and all the zebras shaking
themselves in various ways to get rid of their stripes in a dew of fresh
milk.

Et au milieu de tout cela je dis hurrah ! mon grand père meurt, je dis
hurrah
la vieille négritude progressivement se cadavérise.
Il n'y a pas à dire : c'était un bon nègre.
Les Blancs disent que c'était un bon nègre, un vrai bon nègre, le bon
nègre à son bon maître.
Je dis hurrah !
C'était un très bon nègre
la misère lui avait blessé poitrine et dos et on avait fourré dans sa pauvre
cervelle qu'une fatalité pesait sur lui qu'on ne prend pas au collet ; qu'il
n'avait pas puissance sur son propre destin ; qu'un Seigneur méchant
avait de toute éternité écrit des lois d'interdiction en sa nature pelvienne ;
et d'être le bon nègre ; de se contenter honnêtement d'être le bon nègre ;
de croire honnêtement à son indignité, sans curiosité perverse de vérifier
les hiéroglyphes fatidiques.

C'était un très bon nègre

et il ne lui venait pas à l'idée qu'il pourrait houer, fouir, couper tout tout
autre chose vraiment que la canne insipide.

C'était un très bon nègre.

Et on lui jetait des pierres, des bouts de ferraille, des tessons de bouteille,
mais ni ces pierres, ni cette ferraille, ni ces bouteilles. . .
O quiètes années de Dieu sur cette motte terraquée !

Et le fouet disputa au bombillement des mouches la rosée sucrée de nos
plaies

And in the midst of all that I say hurray! my grandfather dies, I say hurray
the old negritude progressively cadavers itself.
No bones about it: he was a good nigger.
The Whites say he was a good nigger, a really good nigger, massa's good ole darky.
I say hurray!
He was a good nigger indeed
poverty had wounded his chest and back and they had stuffed into his poor brain that a fatality no one could trap weighed on him; that he had no control over his own destiny; that an evil Lord had for all eternity in-scribed Thou Shall Not in his pelvic constitution; that he must be a good nigger; must honestly put up with being a good nigger; must sincerely believe in his worthlessness, without any perverse curiosity to verify the fatidic hieroglyphs.

[98]

He was a very good nigger

[99]

And it never occurred to him that he could hoe, dig, cut anything, any-thing else really than insipid cane.

[100]

He was a very good nigger.

[101]

And they threw stones at him, chunks of scrap iron, shards of bottles, but neither these stones, nor this scrap iron, nor these bottles . . .
O peaceful years of God on this terraqueous clod!

[102]

And the whip argued with the bombilation of the flies over the sugary dew of our sores

[103]
Je dis hurrah ! La vieille négritude progressivement se cadavérise
l'horizon se défait, recule et s'élargit
et voici parmi des déchiquètements de nuages la fulgurance d'un signe
le négrier craque de toute part. . . Son ventre se convulse et résonne. . .
L'affreux ténia de sa cargaison ronge les boyaux fétides de l'étrange
nourrisson des mers !

[104]
Et ni l'allégresse des voiles gonflées comme une poche de doublons rebon-
die, ni les tours joués à la sottise dangereuse des frégates policières ne
l'empêchent d'entendre la menace de ses grondements intestins.

[105]
En vain pour s'en distraire le capitaine pend à sa grand'vergue le nègre le
plus braillard ou le jette à la mer, ou le livre à l'appétit de ses molosses.

[106]
La négraille aux senteurs d'oignon frit retrouve dans son sang répandu le
goût amer de la liberté

[107]
Et elle est debout la négraille

[108]
la négraille assise
inattendument debout
debout dans la cale
debout dans les cabines
debout sur le pont
debout dans le vent
debout sous le soleil
debout dans le sang
    debout
        et
           libre
debout et non point pauvre folle dans sa liberté et son dénuement mari-
times girant en la dérive parfaite

I say hurray! The old negritude progressively cadavers itself
the horizon breaks, recoils and expands
and through the shredding of clouds the flashing of a sign
the slave ship cracks from one end to the other . . . Its belly convulses and
resounds . . . The ghastly tapeworm of its cargo gnaws the fetid guts of
the strange suckling of the sea!

And neither the joy of sails filled like a pocket stuffed with doubloons, nor
the tricks played on the dangerous stupidity of the patrol ships prevent it
from hearing the threat of its intestinal rumblings.

In vain to amuse himself the captain hangs the biggest loudmouth nigger
from the main yard or throws him into the sea, or feeds him to his mastiffs.

Reeking of fried onions the nigger scum discovers in its spilled blood the
bitter taste of freedom

And the nigger scum is on its feet

the seated nigger scum
unexpectedly standing
standing in the hold
standing in the cabins
standing on the deck
standing in the wind
standing under the sun
standing in the blood
    standing
         and
            free
standing and no longer a poor creature in its maritime freedom and
destitution gyrating in perfect drift

et la voici :
plus inattendument debout
debout dans les cordages
debout à la barre
debout à la boussole
debout à la carte
debout sous les étoiles
    debout
        et
            libre
et le navire lustral s'avancer impavide sur les eaux écroulées.
Et maintenant tombent
et maintenant pourrissent nos flocs d'ignominie

[109]
à moi mes danses
mes danses de mauvais nègre
la danse brise-carcan
la danse saute-prison
la danse il-est-beau-et-bon-et-légitime-d'être-nègre
À moi mes danses et saute le soleil sur la raquette de mes mains
Mais non l'inégal soleil ne me suffit plus
enroule-toi, vent, autour de ma nouvelle croissance
pose-toi sur mes doigts mesurés
Je te livre ma conscience et son rythme de chair
Je te livre les feux où brasille ma faiblesse
Je te livre le chain-gang
Je te livre le marais
Je te livre l'in-tourist du circuit triangulaire
Dévore vent
Je te livre mes paroles abruptes
Dévore et enroule-toi
Et t'enroulant embrasse-moi d'un plus vaste frisson
Embrasse-moi jusqu'au nous furieux
Embrasse, embrasse NOUS
Mais nous ayant également mordus !
Jusqu'au sang de notre sang mordus !

54

and there it is:
most unexpectedly standing
standing in the rigging
standing at the tiller
standing at the compass
standing at the map
standing under the stars
    standing
        and
           free
and the lustral ship advances fearlessly over the crumbling waters.
And now our ignominious plops
are falling and rotting away

[109]

rally to my side my dances
my bad-nigger dances
the carcan-break dance
the prison-spring dance
the it-is-beautiful-good-and-legitimate-to-be-a-nigger-dance
Rally to my side my dances and let the sun bounce on the racket of my
hands
But no the unequal sun is not enough for me
coil, wind, around my new growth
light on my cadenced fingers
To you I surrender my conscience and its fleshy rhythm
To you I surrender the fire in which my weakness sparkles
To you I surrender the chain gang
To you the swamps
To you the non-tourist of the triangular circuit
Devour wind
To you I surrender my abrasive words
Devour and encoil yourself
And coiling round embrace me with a more ample shudder
Embrace me unto furious us
Embrace, embrace US
But having also bitten us!
To the blood of our blood bitten us!

Embrasse, ma pureté ne se lie qu'à ta pureté
mais alors embrasse !
Comme un champ de justes filaos
le soir
nos multicolores puretés.
Et lie, lie-moi sans remords
lie-moi de tes vastes bras à l'argile lumineuse
lie ma noire vibration au nombril même du monde
Lie, lie-moi, fraternité âpre
Puis, m'étranglant de ton lasso d'étoiles
monte, Colombe
monte
monte
monte
Je te suis, imprimée en mon ancestrale cornée blanche
Monte lécheur de ciel
Et le grand trou noir où je voulais me noyer l'autre lune
C'est là que je veux pêcher maintenant
la langue maléfique de la nuit en son immobile verrition !

Embrace, my purity mingles only with your purity
so then embrace!
Like a field of upright filaos
at dusk
our multicolored purities.
And bind, bind me without remorse
bind me with your vast arms of luminous clay
bind my black vibration to the very navel of the world
Bind, bind me, bitter brotherhood
Then, strangling me with your lasso of stars
rise, Dove
rise
rise
rise
I follow you who are imprinted on my ancestral white cornea
Rise sky licker
And the great black hole where a moon ago I wanted to drown
It is there I will now fish
the malevolent tongue of the night in its still verticity*!

Appendix: Césaire's *Cahier* in Translation

Comments on the Translations

The present translation by A. James Arnold and Clayton Eshleman has been realized after careful study of the 1939 French text. It is a substantially new translation based on the one Eshleman did with Annette Smith in the late 1970s, before revising it for *Aimé Césaire: The Collected Poetry* (1983) and the 2001 Wesleyan University Press edition of *Notebook of a Return to the Native Land*. The Eshleman and Smith translation and its later revisions were based on the 1976 edition of Césaire's *Poésie*, edited by Jean Paul Césaire for Désormeaux (Fort-de-France and Paris). René Hénane's glossary of rare words in Césaire's oeuvre has allowed for substantial improvement in the treatment of lexical difficulties. Germain Kouassi's monograph on Césaire's language and style in the *Notebook* has been helpful in identifying characteristic syntactical structures. Abiola Irele's annotated edition of a version of the 1956 Présence Africaine text has frequent helpful insights. Lilyan Kesteloot published a guide to the *Cahier / Notebook* for student readers in 1983. Kesteloot has found biblical echoes in the text that reinforce our reading of the poem as a spiritual drama. Other references can be found following the notes.

The first English translation of Césaire's poem, *Memorandum on My Martinique*, by Abel and Goll, has never been reprinted. Émile Snyder used it as the starting point for his translation, which was published as *Return to My Native Land* in a bilingual edition published by Présence Africaine in Paris (1971) and long out of print. The Snyder translation has the peculiarity of not corresponding perfectly to the post-1956 French text on the facing page since Snyder worked from an earlier draft. In the United Kingdom there have been two translations, the first as *Return to My Native Land* by Berger and Bostock for Penguin (1969); the introduction by Masizi Kunene oriented the translation sharply toward Africa. Until publication of the Eshleman–Smith translation in 1983, the *Notebook* was read quite consistently through an Africanist political lens. In 1995 Bloodaxe

Books published a bilingual edition with a translation by Annie Pritchard and Mireille Rosello. Rosello's introduction sets Césaire's poem in a postcolonial perspective.

Césaire consulted with Janheinz Jahn on lexical difficulties of his German translation, which Insel-Verlag in Frankfurt published in 1962 as *Zurück ins Land der Geburt*. Moreover, Jahn's activity on Césaire's behalf from the mid-1950s to the mid-1960s did much to popularize the Martinican poet. Césaire prefaced the Paris edition of Jahn's book *Muntu*, which drew Césaire into the orbit of the one-black-world ideology of the 1960s that fixed the image of Negritude for half a century.

The Lydia Cabrera translation, published in Havana as *Retorno al país natal* early in 1943 with illustrations by Wifredo Lam resulted directly from Lam's meeting with Césaire in Fort-de-France in 1941. Their mutual admiration nurtured a forty-year friendship that ended with Lam's death in 1982. The Cabrera translation enjoys the distinction of being the first edition of Césaire's poem in book form, appearing four years prior to the original edition in French. In 2007 Lourdes Arencibia published in Zamora, Spain a hybrid text of the Havana *Retorno* . . . to which she added, in her own Spanish translation, material from the 1956 Présence Africaine edition. Enrique Lihn prepared a second Cuban translation of the *Cahier* for a volume of Césaire's *Poesías*, prefaced by René Depestre and published in Havana at Casa de las Américas (1956). Agustí Bartra's translation of *Cuaderno de un retorno al país natal* was published in Mexico City by Era in 1969. In 1995 Consuelo Gotay illustrated this translation with engravings in a limited edition published in San Juan, Puerto Rico.

Graziano Benelli, who championed Césaire in Italy, published his translation of *Diario di un retorno al paese natale* in Milan in 1978. In 1985 the Dutch publisher In de Knipscheer, which has specialized in titles from the Netherlands Antilles, published Simon Simonse's translation in Haarlem under the title *Logboek van een Terugkeer naar Mijn Geboorteland*. This Dutch translation made Césaire's poem available in the fourth major European language of the Caribbean region.

Notes on the Translation

[4] *the volcanoes will explode*: In May 1902 Mt. Pelée exploded pyroclastically, burying the old colonial capital of Martinique, St. Pierre, in volcanic ash. Metaphorically volcanoes and explosions set up a network of apocalyptic images that run through the poem.

[8] *Joséphine ... conquistador*: Césaire presents ironically three statues that collectively represent the official history of colonization. Marie-Josèphe-Rose Tascher de la Pagerie (1763–1814), born at La Pagerie near Trois-Îlets, Martinique, was called Joséphine by her second husband, Napoleon I. Martinicans blame her for encouraging Napoleon to reinstitute slavery in 1802. Her statue has frequently been decapitated in recent years. Victor Schoelcher (1804–1893) is credited with the abolition of slavery in the French Empire by the revolutionary government in 1848. In 1939 Schoelcherism in the French West Indies was a mythic construct intended to convince blacks that freedom was given to them by magnanimous whites. Césaire opposes this passive myth to the revolutionary history of Haiti. Pierre Belain d'Esnambuc (1585–1636) was a Norman French privateer to whom Richelieu accorded the privilege of colonizing the islands of the Lesser Antilles that were then unoccupied by Europeans. He is remembered without affection as the founder of French colonialism in the Caribbean region.

[10] *morne*: Lafcadio Hearn, in *Two Years* . . . , defined the term as "used through the French West Indies to designate certain altitutes (usually with beautiful and curious forms) of volcanic origin . . ." Césaire connects this evocative term both with the poverty of the island and with the apocalyptic explosion that may one day bring it to an end.

[14] *suicide*: Slaves sometimes committed suicide by choking on their own tongues (the hypoglossal nerves are at the base of the tongue).

[14] The *Capot River* empties into the Atlantic Ocean in Basse-Terre, Martinique, where Césaire was born. Its course is Southeast of the plantation where his father served as manager before entering the colonial tax department.

[15] *Queen-Blanche-of-Castille*: Daughter of Eleanor of Aquitaine, wife of Louis VIII of France and mother of Louis IX, Blanche (1188–1252) figured prominently in school history books. She probably appears in the poem both as a synecdoche of the irrelevance of medieval French history to colonials and as a privileged metaphor of the whiteness attaching to her name.

[21] *Trinité to Grand-Rivière*: From Césaire's boyhood home, Basse-Terre, La Trinité lies to the South, Grand-Rivière to the North, along the wild Atlantic coast, which faces Africa.

[26] MERCI: THANK YOU; an ex-voto for an answered prayer. Césaire's paternal grandmother, Eugénie Macni, was educated by her common-law husband. She in turn instructed her grandchildren before they entered school. Césaire maintained that she looked like the Diola people of Casamance in Senegal.

[27] *Straw Street*: In French, *rue Paille*; the poorest shacks in the colony lacked the solid roof of more prosperous houses.

[28] *sand so black*: These images reinforce the poverty of the black population. The sand is black because of its volcanic origin.

[31] *three-souled Carib*: Césaire refers to the three aspects of the person in Carib belief: *anigi* (vital force); *iuani* (immaterial being); *afurugu* (astral body). The astral body is an exact copy of the physical body and is located midway between materiality and spirituality.

[32] *little ellipsoidal nothing*: A derisive designation for Martinique, which is finger-like in shape. At only 1,100 sq. km., it is approximately six times the size of Washington, D.C. Located at 14.40 degrees North Latitude, it would appear to lie four fingers above the equator on a medium-sized wall map.

[34] *where negritude rose for the first time*: This is the first intimation that Negritude should be seen as a heroic opposition to the diminished sense of self inculcated by colonization. In the poem Haiti stands for all that colonized Martinique is not. When they designate the sick, corrupt society that has resulted from three centuries of colonization, images of blackness are translated using terms, however offensive, that show the unacceptable nature of present reality.

where Death scythes widely: This is probably an allusion to the Spanish Civil War, which ended in a fascist victory while Césaire was composing the "Notebook . . ." Franco's armies invaded Spain from its African colonies using tanks that can be seen as "caterpillaring . . ."

[35] *Bordeaux . . . San Francisco*: All but the last city participated in the triangle trade: goods from French and British ports were traded for slaves on the African coast; slave ships traded their human cargo in the West Indies and the plantation economies of Atlantic America; rum and sugar were sent back to Europe from American and Caribbean ports. San Francisco seems to have been added for euphony and rhythm.

[36] *a little cell in the Jura*: Toussaint Louverture (1743–1803) was the foremost military hero of the Haitian revolution, which inflicted its worst defeat on Napoleon's armies prior to the debacle of 1812 in Russia. Césaire considered the black revolution to be the dialectical end-point of a struggle that began with the revolt of the white planters, was opposed by the parliamentary struggle of the mulattoes during the French Revolution, and concluded with the proclamation of the black republic in 1804. He devoted a historical essay to Toussaint Louverture in 1960 and a play to King Henry Christophe in 1963, making Haiti a centerpiece of his depiction of Negritude, which he modified over time. In the "Notebook . . ." he focuses on Toussaint's destiny as a tragic sacrifice. Toussaint was tricked by the French into coming on board a man-of-war in 1802, was

imprisoned and transported to the Fort de Joux in the Jura Mountains, where he died a miserable death a year later.

the Keys: Caribbean coral reefs.

shy patyura: According to Césaire, a variation on *patira*, the name of a peccary found in French Guiana. According to Kesteloot, it is also thought to accompany the dying to their final resting place; in this respect it would be a Creole equivalent to the Egyptian Anubis.

[49] *Amazons*: The kings of precolonial Dahomey maintained a unit of women warriors who cut off one breast to facilitate archery in battle.

Askia the Great: Askia Mohammed reigned in Gao from 1493 to 1528; he founded the university at Timbuktu.

Djenne: A city of precolonial Mali famous for its Great Mosque. From the fifteenth to the seventeenth century Djenne was a major link in trading salt and gold through Timbuktu. If Césaire knew that slaves were also traded there, he doesn't mention it.

Madhi: In Muslim eschatology, the madhi is a prophet guided by Allah who is destined to save the faithful at world's end. In recent history Muhammad Ahmad ibn Abd Allah Al-Mahdi (1844–1885) led an insurrection in the Anglo-Egyptian Sudan. The state he founded survived him until 1898, when the British army under Lord Kitchener destroyed it.

Chicote: A Portuguese knotted whip used on slaves.

[52] This strophe is a tissue of allusions to the claims of so-called scientific racism, of which Joseph Arthur de Gobineau (1816–1882) was the foremost exponent in France. His book *The Inequality of Human Races*, first published between 1853 and 1855, contributed significantly to the theory of innate European superiority that justified the subjugation of non-European peoples by the colonial powers. Measuring skull size with a craniometer was a favorite means of proving superiority or inferiority. *Homo sum* . . . may be a quotation from Terence, the Roman author who was born a slave to a senator. Kesteloot reads this quotation as an ironic rejoinder to the fate reserved for African and diasporic peoples by colonial racism.

COMICAL AND UGLY: A quotation from Charles Baudelaire's poem "The Albatross," which depicts this majestic bird as pathetic when confined to the deck of a ship by cruel sailors. The parallel with the black man on the streetcar is intended to show his present degradation as the direct result of his circumstances. The speaker's ironic assumption of racist stereotypes while looking at him calls for translation of *nègre* as *nigger*. In this sequence the speaker must overcome his own racist conditioning.

[53] *funereal menfenil*: Any number of Caribbean raptors have been identified under this common name. Jourdain identified the *menfenil* (Creole: *malfini*) as *Falco sparverius caribaearum*, the sparrow hawk or kestrel. Pompilus thought it must be *Accipiter stiratus*, a local sharp-shinned hawk. Hénane preferred an endemic Martinican species, *Buteo playtypterus rivieri*, a local broad-winged hawk. Valdman may have been right to call it "chicken hawk," which is no known bird but rather any raptor that threatens the chickens. Césaire's metonymic purpose is clear, however. His hawk is dark (funereal) and threatening. Thibault discusses all these possibilities going back to the 1660s, without reaching a clear conclusion.

[57] *postillion*: A household servant dressed in fancy livery whose job it was to tell the newly-arrived slaves, in flowery language, what a fine life awaited them in Havana.

[66] *Eia . . . Cailcedra*: Eia is an imperative that is found both in ancient Greek drama and in the Latin missal. "Eia Mater" occurs in the prayer "Stabat Mater dolorosa." Either association reinforces the solemnity of the context in the poem. In the Wolof language of Senegal, Cailcedra designates an African mahogany tree. Senghor also used the word in his poetry.

[67] *but who yield, seized, to the essence of all things*: Césaire here gives central importance to a fundamental thesis of his mentor in the morphology of cultures, Leo Frobenius. In the first issue of *Tropiques* (April 1941) Suzanne Césaire explained these characteristics of the so-called Ethiopian peoples of Africa with whom she and her husband identified. See Suzanne Césaire, *The Great Camouflage: Writings of Dissent (1941–1945)*, ed. by Daniel Maximin, trans. by Keith L. Walker (Middletown, Conn.: Wesleyan University Press, 2012), 3–10.

[78] *the time has come to gird one's loins like a brave man*: In the Book of Job (38:3) Jehovah enjoins Job: "Gird up now thy loins like a man" (King James trans.). The context is God's laying the foundations of the earth.

[82] *the wounds cut in its trunk*: A probable allusion to the rubber tree, which survives the incisions made in its trunk for collection of latex sap.

[87] *I am only a man (no degradation, no spit perturbs him)*: Echoes the scourging of Christ; Matthew and Mark stress spitting; John (19:5) has the expression "Behold the man!" (*Ecce Homo* in the Vulgate).

I accept . . . I accept . . . totally, without reservation . . .: Kesteloot sees here an allusion to the gospel according to Luke (22:42): "not my will, but thine, be done."

my race that no ablution of hyssop mixed with lilies could purify: The line echoes Psalm 51:7 ("Purge me with hyssop, and I shall be clean: wash me, and I shall be whiter than snow.") Irele sees a more elaborate network of metaphors:

"hyssop is an aromatic plant mentioned in the Latin chant (beginning with the words *Asperges me*) that accompanies the ritual sprinkling of the congregation with holy water before High Mass in the Catholic Church . . ." He adds that the lily is "the emblem of the Bourbon monarchy in France. An intimate connection is thus established between the general system of references within Western culture and the symbolism of the Church which, as its principal component, the symbolism helps to sustain" (p. 127).

my race ripe grapes for drunken feet: In Isaiah 63:3 Jehovah declares: "I have trodden the winepress alone; and of the people there was none with me: for I will tread them in mine anger, and trample them in my fury . . ."

(oh those queens . . . chestnut trees!): Quite possibly an allusion to the statues of French queens in the Luxembourg Gardens in Paris, one of whom is Blanche of Castille. The parenthetical ejaculation is reminiscent of the style of Saint-John Perse.

the twenty-nine legal blows of the whip: Here and in naming instruments of torture below Césaire draws upon the *Code Noir* (Black Code) written by Colbert, Louis XIV's minister, in 1685 and revised many times down to the abolition of slavery in 1848. Césaire documented the names of slaveholders who exacted particularly cruel punishments in the writings of Victor Schoelcher. In 1948 for the centennial of abolition Césaire prefaced *Esclavage et Colonisation* (Slavery and Colonialism), which collected Schoelcher's principal essays on the subject. The chapter on "La condition servile" (The servile state) is particularly apposite here.

and the fleur de lys: Branding irons bearing this symbol of the monarchy were used to mark runaway slaves who had been recaptured.

[89] *and the determination of my biology*: All these measures of racial purity up to "but measured" refer to the tests established by "scientific" racism and which were, all too often, interiorized by black and mulatto families in plantation society.

[92] *the body of my country miraculously laid in the despair of my arms*: Replication of the biblical scene in which Joseph of Arimathaea takes the body of Christ down from the cross (Luke 23:52–53).

and I revive Onan: In Genesis 38:9 Onan refused to impregnate his dead brother's widow. When Jehovah saw that Onan had disobeyed the divine injunction, He killed Onan. As he does elsewhere, Césaire keeps the vehicle of the metaphor (the speaker will copulate with Mother Earth) but provides a new tenor (a nature religion that harks back to Africa).

[93] *the penetrance of an apocalyptic wasp*: A probable allusion to the book

of Revelation (*Apocalypse* in French), in which the end-times are announced by locust armies having the power of scorpions to cause men pain and suffering (Revelation 9:3–10). Kesteloot sees the aural image as referencing the trumpet of the angel of the Last Judgment.

[96] *the "lance of night" of my Bambara ancestors*: Kesteloot glosses this tutelary image as the *sutama*, a spear blessed by a sorcerer who sprinkled it with the blood of a man or a black goat. Without the blessing the spear would retract toward the haft so as to be ineffective. The Bambara or Bamana are a Mandé people whose range extends from Mali to Senegal. A subgroup of the Mandé founded Djenne around 250 BC. Other subgroups founded the Ghana Empire prior to 1100 AD and the songhai empire, which dissolved around 1600 AD. Césaire's image then conveys both warlike and imperial connotations.

pseudomorphosis: When Césaire published the preoriginal of the "Notebook . . ." in 1939, debates over Oswald Spengler's notion of pseudomorphosis were common. Spengler found the term in Frobenius, who had used it in a discussion of the mysterious force of Païdeuma, which seized cultures and transformed them. Spengler interpreted pseudomorphosis as the cultural crippling of a young society by an older one. Césaire in the "Notebook . . ." imputes the physical and moral ills of Martinican society to the imposition of Western institutions on a diasporic people he sees as African. Césaire's use of biblical images to suggest a narrative of spiritual salvation may owe something to Spengler's claim that "everywhere 'he,' the son of man, the savior who has descended into the underworld and who must himself be saved, is the hoped-for goal. . . . Apocalyptic thought . . . henceforth fills his consciousness entirely" (vol. 2, 197–98).

pay no attention to my black skin: the sun did it: In the Song of Solomon (1:6) one reads: "Look not upon me, because I am black, because the sun hath looked upon me . . ." In the context of pseudomorphosis, this is a denial of blackness, which Fanon was to theorize in *Black Skin, White Masks*.

[109] *still verticity*: In the French text *verrition* is a Latinism that Césaire explained to Eshleman and Smith as coined from the verb *verri*: to sweep, scrape a surface, to scan. Kesteloot, who had also consulted Césaire, claimed the root was *vertere*, to turn. André Claverie was given the same etymology by Césaire. Hénane found *verrition* as a culinary term in Brillat-Savarin's *Physiologie du goût* (1825) and interpreted the image as the tongue sweeping bits of food in the mouth. We agree with Kesteloot that the poetic sense of the image is an arrested turning motion. We have settled on the translation "still verticity" to render that meaning while suggesting the powerful upward sweep of the final passage.

Works Cited

Hearn, Lafcadio. 1890. *Two Years in the French West Indies*. New York: Harper and Brothers.

Hénane, René. 2004. *Glossaire des termes rares dans l'oeuvre d'Aimé Césaire*. Paris: Jean-Michel Place.

Irele, Francis Abiola, ed. 1994. *Cahier d'un retour au pays natal* by Aimé Césaire. Ibadan, Nigeria: New Horn Press; 2nd edition 2000. Columbus: Ohio State University Press.

Jourdain, Élodie. 1956. *Le vocabulaire du parler créole de la Martinique*. Paris: Klincksieck.

Kesteloot, Lilyan. 1983. *Comprendre* Cahier d'un retour au pays natal *d'Aimé Césaire*. Versailles: Les Classiques Africains.

Kouassi, Germain. 2006. *La Poésie de Césaire par la langue et le style: l'exemple du* "Cahier d'un retour au pays natal." Lettres & Langues. Paris: Publibook.

Spengler, Oswald. 1932. *The Decline of the West*, trad. de C.F. Atkinson. Vol. 2. *Perspectives of World-History*. London; New York: Allen & Unwin; Knopf [1928].

Thibault, André. 2008. "L'œuvre d'Aimé Césaire et le français régional antillais." In *Aimé Césaire à l'oeuvre*, ed. Marc Cheymol and Philippe Ollé-Laprune, 47–85. Paris: Archives Contemporaines.

A Césaire Chronology

1913   Birth of Aimé Fernand David Césaire on June 26 in Basse-Pointe, Martinique, where his father managed a sugarcane plantation. The official date is June 25.

1924   Family moves to Fort-de-France, the colonial capital, after Fernand Césaire enters the colonial tax department, substantially improving the family's prospects.

1924–31   Secondary education at the Lycée Schoelcher, where L.-G. Damas from Guyana is also a student.

1931–35   Scholarship student at the Lycée Louis-le-Grand in Paris, where he undergoes intense preparation for the École Normale Supérieure (ENS), which has formed the intellectual elite of France since Napoleon I founded it. Meets L. S. Senghor and has his first contact with colonial African students.

1935   In March assumes editorship of Martinican student paper, which he renames *L'Étudiant noir*. His original proposal, *L'Étudiant nègre*, is refused by fellow Martinicans, who find it injurious. Senghor joins him in opening the paper to broader examination of the condition of black students who are attacked, morally in the press and physically in the streets, by fascists. Both the concept and the word *Négritude* first appear here.

    Succeeds against general expectation in the entrance examination for ENS, but experiences exhaustion and depression over the summer, which he spends with Petar Guberina on the Adriatic coast of Croatia. View of the island of Martiniska triggers memories of home that Césaire begins to transfer to a notebook.

1936   First return to Martinique in five years during summer vacation. In December, in a state of heady enthusiasm, reads L. Frobenius's *Histoire de la civilisation africaine* (History of African Civilization) with Senghor.

1937	Marries Suzanne Roussi, a student at the University of Toulouse and friend of his sister Mireille, in July. The couple moves into student quarters at the ENS where the first of their six children is born.
1938	Césaire reads a draft of his long poem aloud to L.-G. Damas; some think it was turned down by one or more publishers during this period.
1939	Professor Petitbon at ENS recommends his student's poem to the editor of the avant-garde magazine *Volontés*, which publishes the "Notebook" in the August issue, its last. Césaire writes a new, more definitive conclusion at the editor's suggestion. Senghor has a poem in the same issue, which also publishes translations of poems by Vallejo, Paz, and Neruda.
	Césaire fails the final examinations at the ENS, blaming his lack of concentration on his writing. He returns to Martinique, only weeks after his poem appears, with offprints that will prove invaluable in launching his career as a poet.
1939–41	Aimé Césaire makes a profound impression on students at the Lycée Schoelcher, to which he returned as a teacher of literature and classics after an eight-year absence.
1941	In April, the first issue of *Tropiques* is published by the Césaires and several of their colleagues. A freighter chartered in Marseille by the Varian Fry group who helped intellectuals and artists escape occupied France deposits André Breton, Wifredo Lam, Claude Lévi-Strauss and others in Fort-de-France for an extended stay. A reading of the "Notebook" has a galvanizing effect on Lam, who undertakes to publish a Spanish translation in Havana. Breton's chance discovery of Césaire's poem "The Thoroughbreds" in *Tropiques* encourages him to take the younger poet under his wing as part of the internationalization of surrealism.
1942–43	In late 1942 Breton receives from Césaire a completely revised version of the *Notebook*, for which he writes the preface "A Great Negro Poet." Originally scheduled to be published bilingually in 1943 by Brentano's in New York, the *Cahier / Notebook* is issued four years later.
	Poems collected under the title *The Miraculous Weapons* (*Les Armes miraculeuses*) in 1946 are published through the efforts of Breton and other surrealists in New York and throughout the western hemisphere.
1943	Lydia Cabrera's translation of the 1939 "Notebook" is published for the first time in book form as *Retorno al país natal* with a preface by Benjamin Péret and three line drawings by Wifredo Lam.

1944	Invited to Port-au-Prince, Haiti, for a stay of several months, Césaire reads a paper on "Poetry and Knowledge" at an international conference on epistemology. The text, his Ars Poetica for the 1940s, is published in *Cahiers d'Haïti* in December 1944. A few weeks later an edited version appears in *Tropiques*.
1945	At the first elections after the war Césaire is elected the Communist mayor of Fort-de-France and Deputy from Central Martinique to the French National Assembly.
1946	Césaire co-sponsors the law that ends colonial status for the French West Indies and Reunion Island.
	Breton's publisher Gallimard issues *Les Armes miraculeuses*, which reveals Césaire's poetry to the French for the first time, the 1939 "Notebook" having gone unnoticed in France.
1947	In January Brentano's publishes in New York the version of the *Notebook* Césaire had revised in 1942. In March a substantially different version, completed as much as four years later, is published in Paris by Bordas. For decades it was thought the two were identical; André Breton prefaced them both.
	Césaire gives moral support to Alioune Diop who founds the magazine and publishing house Présence Africaine, but he does not publish with them for another nine years.
1948	Césaire's second major poetry collection *Solar Throat Slashed* (*Soleil cou coupé*) is published by K, which specializes in surrealism. Sartre's essay "Black Orpheus" prefaces Senghor's anthology of new poetry from Africa and the diaspora; it will remain in print for at least half a century and will have a major influence on readings of Césaire's poetry.
1949	Publication of *Lost Body* (*Corps perdu*) with thirty-two engravings by Picasso in a limited edition for collectors.
1950	Publication of *Discourse on Colonialism* (*Discours sur le colonialisme*), whose polemical condemnation of colonialism and the racism attendant upon it gives a strong sociopolitical slant to readings of Césaire's poetry.
1956	Césaire joins the Présence Africaine publishing house in June with a heavily revised edition of the *Notebook* that adds new sociopolitical material and minimizes the use of surrealist metaphor that had characterized the two 1947 editions. Petar Guberina, a friend from Césaire's student days and a Yugoslav university professor, prefaces the volume. The back cover of the edition for the first time frames the

Notebook as a clearly African poem. Subsequent editions of the *Note-book* present minor changes.

Présence Africaine issues a revised edition of the *Discourse on Co-lonialism* and publishes the first theatrical version of *And the Dogs Were Silent*. Gallimard keeps the oratorio version as part of *The Mi-raculous Weapons* through the 1971 edition.

"Culture and Colonialism" ("Culture et colonisation") powerfully re-inforces the main points of the *Discourse* when Césaire reads it at the first congress of Negro writers and artists in the Sorbonne in Septem-ber. It receives considerable coverage in the press.

In October he resigns from the Communist Party of France in a re-sounding open *Letter to Maurice Thorez*, the First Secretary. Césaire's letter, composed before the Soviets crushed the Hungarian uprising, responds to deeper and long-standing grievances over the party's atti-tude toward decolonization and ethnicity.

1958   Césaire founds an independent Martinican Progressive Party (PPM), affiliated in the French legislature with the Socialists. He continues to serve as Deputy from Central Martinique until retirement in 1993.

1960   Césaire publishes *Ferraments* (*Ferrements*), a collection written in the previous decade, which puts the new sociopolitical stamp on his poet-ics. His historical essay on Toussaint Louverture reinforces the notion that his poetry and politics share an identical vision.

1961   In editing *Solar Throat Slashed* for his new collection, *Cadaster* (*Ca-dastre*), which also includes *Lost Body*, Césaire cuts out thirty-one of the most markedly surrealist poems and rewrites twenty-nine others to bring them into line with his new poetics. From this date until the Wesleyan University Press bilingual edition in 2011, the original *Solar Throat Slashed* is effectively forgotten.

1963   Césaire's play *The Tragedy of King Christophe* (*La Tragédie du roi Christophe*) examines the risks run by a newly independent black re-public, holding up Haiti under King Christophe as a mirror to new African states. He takes a critical approach to the lyrical and heroic version of Negritude he had championed two decades earlier.

1966   Seuil, which in 1960 became the publisher of his new poetry apart from the *Notebook*, issues Césaire's play *A Season in the Congo* (*Une Saison au Congo*), in which he treats the fate of Patrice Lumumba and the rise of Mobutu Sesi Seku as a tragi-comedy.

1969   In his adaptation of Shakespeare's *Tempest* for a black theater published by Seuil, Césaire interprets Caliban as a revolutionary Malcolm X and Ariel as an accommodating Martin Luther King Jr.

1976   Désormeaux (Paris and Fort-de-France) publishes an expensive three-volume edition of Césaire's *Oeuvres complètes* edited by his son Jean Paul.

1982   A new poetry collection, *moi, laminaire. . .* published by Seuil, takes an elegiac approach to the problems Césaire had addressed aggressively forty years earlier. At the heart of the collection is a series of seven poems that comment on engravings by Wifredo Lam, who was very ill during this final collaboration. Lam dies in 1982.

1983   Présence Africaine publishes a new French edition of the *Notebook* with Breton's well-known "A Great Negro Poet" as the afterword. Breton's framing of the poem begins a revision of the anticolonialist stance of the mid-1950s and 1960s. Maximin and Carpentier reproduce this text in their edition of *La Poésie*.

1992   The library of the National Assembly (Bibliothèque de l'Assemblée Nationale) buys the annotated typescript of the "Notebook" used by the printer for *Volontés* in 1939. The typescript contains late manuscript additions and a letter to the editor.

1994   D. Maximin and G. Carpentier publish Césaire's collected *Poésie* at Seuil, including twenty-two new poems under the title *Comme un malentendu de salut*. The edition is annotated except for the 1983 text of the *Notebook*.

2001   In February Césaire presides over his final municipal council meeting as mayor of Fort-de-France. He is eighty-eight years old and has served for fifty-six years. His constituents know him as Papa Aimé.

2005   Césaire as honorary mayor of the city refuses to receive Nicolas Sarkozy because the French government had recently passed a law that called for the recognition of the positive aspects of colonialism.

2008   Césaire dies on April 17 at age ninety-four. Three days later he receives a national funeral in Fort-de-France. Nicolas Sarkozy as President of the Republic participates in laying to rest the Martinican who had refused to receive him three years earlier.

2011   On April 7 Nicolas Sarkozy gives a speech on the steps of the Panthéon, where France honors its great men and women, praising Aimé Césaire and inaugurating the plaque that memorializes the poet-politician.